T0360510

Accounting Regulation in Japan

Little has been published on accounting standards in Japan and how they have developed. The purpose of this study is to construct a historical narrative of the interplay between accounting standards in Japan and theories of regulation.

The authors demonstrate that delegation of the authority for accounting standard setting to the private sector in Japan is incomplete, and thus, the role of the public sector remains important. In the discussion about IFRS implementation in Japan, the movement in the United States, industry opinions, and ideological conflict between fair value versus historical cost play important roles. These elements combined led to the ambiguous coexistence of four sets of accounting standards in Japan. First, by using an explaining-outcome process-tracing method, the authors examine how these sets of standards occurred and explore the significance of each. Second, they deliver an explanation of this unique coexistence through the lens of theories of regulation. In doing so, they provide an overview of the history of the recent development of accounting regulation in Japan and offer an up-to-date response to current affairs or policy debates in Japan that have been rapidly changing.

Providing a rare insight into accounting regulation in Japan, an IFRS non-application country, this concise text will be of great interest to researchers and advanced students in international accounting and accounting regulation.

Masatsugu Sanada, PhD, joined Kyoto Tachibana University in April 2019 as Associate Professor in Accounting, Faculty of Contemporary Business, having previously been Associate Professor at Shujitsu University. Sanada entered the Graduate School of Economics at Kyoto University as a mature student and obtained his PhD in 2012.

Yoshihiro Tokuga, PhD, is a Professor of Accounting at the Graduate School of Management, Kyoto University. He is the President of the Japan Accounting Association, former President of Asian Academic Accounting Association, and former Vice-President of International Association of Accounting Education and Research. He also serves as the Chairman of Business Accounting Council of the Financial Services Agency of Japan.

Routledge Focus on Accounting and Auditing

Advances in the fields of accounting and auditing as areas of research and education, alongside shifts in the global economy present a constantly shifting environment. This presents challenges for scholars and practitioners trying to keep up with the latest important insights in both theory and professional practice. *Routledge Focus on Accounting and Auditing* presents concise texts on key topics in the world of accounting research.

Individually, each title in the series provides coverage of a key topic in accounting and auditing, whilst collectively, the series forms a comprehensive collection across the discipline of accounting.

The Boundaries in Financial and Non-Financial Reporting
A Comparative Analysis of their Constitutive Role
Laura Girella

The Future of Auditing
David Hay

Accounting Regulation in Japan
Evolution and Development from 2001 to 2015
Masatsugu Sanada and Yoshihiro Tokuga

For more information about the series, please visit www.routledge.com/ Routledge-Focus-on-Accounting-and-Auditing/book-series/RFAA

Accounting Regulation in Japan

Evolution and Development from 2001 to 2015

Masatsugu Sanada and Yoshihiro Tokuga

LONDON AND NEW YORK

First published 2020
by Routledge
2 Park Square, Milton Park, Abingdon, Oxon OX14 4RN

and by Routledge
52 Vanderbilt Avenue, New York, NY 10017

Routledge is an imprint of the Taylor & Francis Group, an informa business

British Library Cataloguing-in-Publication Data
A catalogue record for this book is available from the British Library

Library of Congress Cataloging-in-Publication Data
Names: Sanada, Masatsugu, author. | Tokuga, Yoshihiro, 1955– author.
Title: Accounting regulation in Japan : evolution and development
    from 2001–2015 / Masatsugu Sanada and Yoshihiro Tokuga.
Description: Abingdon, Oxon ; New York, NY : Routledge, 2020. |
    Series: Routledge focus on accounting and auditing | Includes
    bibliographical references and index.
Identifiers: LCCN 2019029191 | ISBN 9780367221072 (hardback :
    alk. paper) | ISBN 9780429273261 (e-book)
Subjects: LCSH: Accounting—Standards—Japan—History—21st
    century. | Accounting—Japan—History—21st century.
Classification: LCC HF5616.J3 S26 2020 | DDC 657.02/1852—dc23
LC record available at https://lccn.loc.gov/2019029191

ISBN: 978-0-367-22107-2 (hbk)
ISBN: 978-0-429-27326-1 (ebk)

Typeset in Times New Roman
by Apex CoVantage, LLC

Contents

Conclusions 64

Figures

Tables

Acknowledgments

Like most books, this one would not have been written without the contributions of many researchers. We would like to thank them for making this publication possible. Most of the conceptual ideas originated discussions at Kyoto University with members of Tokuga's seminar. We would like to explicitly thank Toshitake Miyauchi and Tomoaki Yamashita. There are a number of individuals to whom we wish to give special thanks for their critical and highly constructive comments on earlier versions of the manuscript we presented: Carolyn Cordery, Sidney Gray, Stephen Zeff, Eiichiro Kudo, Keiichi Oishi, and Tomomi Shiosaki.

Tokuga gratefully acknowledges the financial support from the Japan Society for the Promotion of Science Grant-in-Aid for Scientific Research (B) (26285100 and 17H02581).

Finally, we would like to express special thanks to editorial team in Routledge, especially for Jacqueline Curthoys and Emmie Shand. Without their help, this project could not be realized.

Introduction

Summary of this book

Motivation

Accounting is shaped by the environment, and jurisdictions that have experienced different types of environmental development follow various accounting system patterns[1] (Gernon & Meek, 2001; Nobes & Parker, 2017). Thus, given these differences in accounting systems, international accounting researchers have focused on accounting classifications (e.g. Doupnik & Salter, 1995; Gray, 1988; Mueller, 1967; Nair & Frank, 1980; Nobes, 1983). However, especially after 2000, the global diffusion of International Financial Reporting Standards (IFRS)[2] has made it possible for jurisdictions with different accounting environments to share common sets of accounting standards and for multiple sets of accounting standards to coexist within a country.

The global harmonization of accounting standards[3] is justified with such discourse as IFRS are a set of transparent, comparative, and high-quality standards, and establishing a global common standard will enhance capital market efficiency (Suzuki, 2012). However, the findings of many empirical studies suggest that the economic consequences of IFRS are still affected by some country-specific environmental factors (i.e. variables) (Ahmed, Chalmers, & Khlif, 2013; Leuz, 2010; Leuz & Wysocki, 2016). Indeed, many country-level case studies find various types of country-specific implementations of IFRS, contrary to the meaning of the term "adoption," and pure IFRS are not always used in place of domestic standards (IFRSF, 2017; UNCTAD, 2008). For instance, Holthausen (2009) describes the current worldwide accounting situation as follows:

> The adoption of IFRS around the world is occurring rapidly under the assumption that there will be benefits from having a uniform set of

standards for financial reporting around the world so that cross-country comparisons of firms are easier and more transparent. However, that goal will not be fully realized unless the underlying institutional and economic factors evolve to become more similar as well, which seems unlikely (or at least more costly and time-consuming than changing accounting standards). Moreover, if the underlying institutional and economic factors do not become similar across countries over time, then the goal of similar financial reporting outcomes is not likely be a desirable economic outcome.

(Holthausen, 2009, pp. 447–448)

Research questions

These circumstances lead us to ask how the global harmonization of accounting standards impacts accounting regulation in local settings. This question motivates our study and is particularly relevant to Japan, where "regulatory competition" (Sunder, 2002) is underway. Specifically, since the late 1990s, Japan's accounting system has changed in the following ways: (1) the setting of accounting standards has switched from the public to the private sector; (2) Japanese generally accepted accounting principles (GAAP) have converged with US GAAP, and, later, with IFRS; (3) IFRS can be voluntarily applied; (4) a Japanese "roadmap" for the mandatory adoption of IFRS has been proposed and postponed; and (5) Japan's Modified International Standards (JMIS) have been endorsed and published. Japan has therefore most recently authorized the use of four accounting standards by Japanese-listed companies for their consolidated financial statements: Japanese GAAP, US GAAP, IFRS, and JMIS (IFRSF, 2016; Tsunogaya & Tokuga, 2015). In other words, Japan serves as a unique case of "evolutional diversity" (Aoki, 2010) in which four sets of accounting standards coexist. However, only a few previous studies have considered the emergence of this regulatory competition and its theoretical implications in depth, and few of these have been published in international journals (Matsubara & Endo, 2018; Tsunogaya, 2016).

Thus, to provide insights regarding our motivating question, we develop the following research questions:

1 What causal process led to the unique coexistence of four sets of consolidated accounting standards in Japan?
2 How can we interpret or explain the role or necessity of each standard (i.e. what are the theoretical implications of this situation)?

Purpose

To answer these questions, this study aims to construct a historical narrative of the interplay between accounting standards in Japan and theories of regulation. For that purpose, we first examine the causal process that brought about the coexistence of four sets of accounting standards in Japan and the significance of each set of standards using the explaining-outcome process-tracing method. Second, we attempt to provide minimally sufficient explanations for this unique coexistence through the lens of theories of regulation. In that sense, in the following chapters, we aim to provide "the presentation of a series of snap-shots, as it were, upon which the reader is expected to exercise his [or her] imagination in constructing the outlines of an organized process of" (Scott, 1931, pp. 3–4) the evolution of contemporary accounting in Japan.

Methodology

To achieve these goals, we use the process-tracing method, which combines a narrative that inductively analyzes historical events with a theoretical approach that deductively analyzes the issues, as our overall analytical strategy. Specifically, we use the explaining-outcome process-tracing approach, which seeks to create "a minimally sufficient explanation of a particular outcome, with sufficiency defined as an explanation that accounts for all of the important aspects of an outcome with no redundant parts being present" (Beach & Pedersen, 2013, p. 18). For its historical account of accounting regulation in Japan, this study focuses on the time period from 2001, when the Accounting Standards Board of Japan (ASBJ) was established, to 2015, when the ASBJ issued JMIS, and we rely on publicly available data that we select and collect from the ASBJ web page and other resources.

We use two analytical techniques in this study. First, we perform a contextual and interpretive analysis of the documents that we collected to reconstruct a historical narrative of accounting regulation in Japan. Second, to develop the theoretical framework of our study, we use a pattern-matching technique (Yin, 2018) to reconstruct three basic categories of regulation theory: public interest theory, capture theory, and cultural theory (or the alternative approach). In so doing, we are strongly inspired and influenced by the works of Allison and Zelikow (1999), which are among the most influential studies of governmental decision making.

Findings

Our historical narrative shows that the Business Accounting Council (BAC) and the ASBJ initially sought mutual recognition and took a cautious approach to the convergence of Japanese GAAP and IFRS. However, the Tokyo Agreement in August 2007 changed the atmosphere, and the situation changed remarkably when the Financial Services Agency (FSA) and the BAC permitted Japanese companies to voluntarily file consolidated financial statements prepared in agreement with IFRS. Some background factors, such as equivalence assessments by the EU and changes in the US's attitude toward IFRS, caused changes in the recognitions of Japanese constituencies. After temporarily taking a cautious stance in 2011 and 2012, the FSA and the BAC regained a positive attitude towards IFRS and sought to create examples of voluntary applications of IFRS with great urgency. At the same time, JMIS were introduced as "a tool" (Tsujiyama, 2014, p. 42) to voice Japan's fundamental ideas regarding the application of IFRS or accounting standards in the international arena.

Our theoretical analysis suggests that that the delegation of authority over accounting standard setting to the private sector is incomplete in Japan, and, thus, the public sector still plays an important role. Although Japan must continue to enhance the quality of Japanese GAAP to achieve the global convergence of accounting standards and ensure Japan's status within the international accounting arena for the public interest in the 2000s, the public sector must also consider the costs to Japanese companies of the continuous changes in accounting standards. Although public and private interests partially conflict and partially coincide, the ASBJ, a private standard setter, is exposed to political pressures from various quarters. Thus, the reformation of accounting regulations in Japan in this era was revolutionary at times and evolutionary at other times in setting a balance between public and private interests.

The Keidanren, one of the most influential pressure groups in Japan, initially took a cautious stance toward the adoption of IFRS. However, as Japanese GAAP and IFRS (and US GAAP) converged and, thus, caused the co-evolution of related institutions, the cost of switching to IFRS, which Japanese companies must bear, has declined. Thus, the Keidanren's attitude has changed, and it has become an active advocate for the adoption of IFRS, leading to further acceleration of the voluntary adoption of IFRS under the Keidanren's initiative.

The coexistence of four sets of accounting standards in Japan appears at first glance to be an ambiguous settlement. However, behind this solution, a conflict between the international school and traditionalists provides some background for this solution. Moreover, as the switching cost has changed as a function of time and environmental changes, ambiguous or extended decisions have resulted in late-comer advantages, and, thus, the coexistence of four accounting standards is rational in some ways.

Value/contributions

This study contributes to the body of knowledge on accounting standards in several ways. First, it contributes to the historical literature. We provide an overview of the history of recent developments of accounting regulations in Japan, with which international readers are not necessarily familiar. Moreover, many historical analyses of Japan take inductive or descriptive approaches (Camfferman & Detzen, 2018; Matsubara & Endo, 2018; Tsunogaya, 2016). Drawing on theories of regulation, we suggest a possible deductive or theory-informed approach to Japan's history.

Second, this study contributes to the comparative literature. Many studies investigate country-specific reactions to the adoption of IFRS (Albu, Albu, & Alexander, 2014; Guerreiro, Rodrigues, & Craig, 2012; Peng & Bewley, 2010) and its economic consequences (Armstrong, Barth, Jagolinzer, & Riedl, 2010; Christensen, Hail, & Leuz, 2013; Daske, Hail, Leuz, & Verdi, 2008, 2013). However, case studies of countries that do not apply IFRS are limited or premature. Thus, this study provides a valuable detailed case study of a country that does not apply IFRS.

Finally, only a few studies have empirically analyzed the specific regulatory competition within a single country. Thus, by providing a timely response to Japan's current affairs and policy debates, which have been rapidly changing, we bridge this gap in the literature by examining Japan's unique experience.

Outline of the chapters

The remainder of this book is organized as follows: the second chapter reviews the prior literature and discusses the theoretical background and methodology of this study. In the third chapter, we address the first research question by tracing the historical development of accounting regulations in Japan and constructing a historical narrative of the unique coexistence of four sets of accounting standards. In the fourth chapter, we address the second research question by discussing the theoretical implications of the Japanese experience through the lens of regulation theory. In the last chapter, we summarize the findings and contributions of this study and indicate directions for future research.

Notes

1 Nobes and Stadler (2013) define an accounting system as "a set of accounting practices, i.e. policies on recognition, measurement and presentation as used in a company's published financial statements" (Nobes & Stadler, 2013, p. 574). However, we extend the term's meaning and include codified rules (i.e. basis

postulates, principles, standards, guidance, and interpretations) along with accounting practices. Although accounting rules and a set of accounting practices comprise an overall accounting system, accounting standards are a salient and significant proxy of an accounting system.

2 In this study, the term "IFRS" connotes International Accounting Standards set by the International Accounting Standards Committee; IFRS, set by the International Accounting Standards Board; and other pronouncements.

3 Generally, the harmonization of accounting standards is perceived as a process of increasing the compatibility of accounting practices by reducing the cross-country differences in the accounting methods allowed under accounting standards and, thus, setting fixed limits on their degree of variation (Tokuga, 2000). "Convergence" refers to the process of converging different standards into a set of benchmark standards, and "adoption" refers to the process of adopting a set of benchmark standards or replacing these standards with domestic standards. In this study, we use the term "harmonization" to mean the integration of the above three processes.

1 Background

Prior literature

International accounting studies

The international harmonization of financial accounting standards has been the main focus of many accounting professionals and researchers for many years. From that perspective, Baker and Barbu (2007) review 202 studies focusing on international accounting harmonization (IAH) published in 24 major English language accounting journals from 1965 to 2004. Their findings demonstrate trends not only in IAH research but also in overall international accounting research (IAR).[1] Specifically, they identify the following trends in IAH research: (1) a significant increase in the number of IAH studies, (2) a significant increase in the use of empirical research methodologies, and (3) an increase in the number of themes in IAH research. They also suggest that these trends will continue in the future, stating that "future IAH research will most likely focus on questions that can be answered through the use of empirical methodologies like those that have been used in the major North American accounting research journals during the last 25 years" (Baker & Barbu, 2007, p. 292).

Christopher Nobes, however, has been leading comparative international accounting studies and international accounting classification studies and continues to actively pursue his research agenda, suggesting that accounting classification remains a valid field of study in the IFRS era (Kvaal & Nobes, 2010; Nobes, 2006, 2008, 2011; Nobes & Stadler, 2013). For instance, Nobes and Stadler (2013) conduct a comprehensive meta-analysis of previous accounting classifications and propose another classification based on IFRS-related decisions. Their findings show that their classifications are highly sensitive to changes in the set of characteristics measured (i.e. the IFRS policy), are not essentially arbitrary, and can be used to support the influence of the frequent dichotomy between common law and code law countries. In particular, they suggest that (1) a classification should be based on detailed observations of characteristics, (2) the selected characteristics should ideally be informed by the purpose of the classification, (3) any claims of objectivity are incoherent, (4) accounting practices represent an accounting system more accurately than rules do, and (5) the set of companies and the period of the data used for the classification should be specified (Nobes & Stadler, 2013, p. 584).

Many international institutions and organizations have conducted surveys of the implementation of IFRS around the world. For example, the International Working Group of Experts on International Standards of Accounting and Reporting of the United Nations Conference on Trade and Development (UNCTAD) conducted detailed case studies of practical implementations of IFRS in eight countries (UNCTAD, 2008). UNCTAD (2008), which indicate that after 2005, an unprecedented number of countries and enterprises around the world adopted IFRS as a global benchmark for the preparation of financial statements and further argues that the benefits of a common set of high-quality accounting standards are significant. However, their case studies also suggest that many countries face several practical challenges, including the incoherence of the regulatory framework, enforcement, and technical capacity.

The IFRS Foundation has developed jurisdictional profiles of IFRS application by surveying 81 jurisdictions, including G20 members. These profiles reveal that 70 jurisdictions (over 85%) have adopted IFRS for at least some companies in their capital markets (IFRSF, 2017). The profiles indicate that few modifications to IFRS are made and that these modifications are generally regarded as temporary steps toward full adoption.

In summary, then, country case studies suggest that pure IFRS are not always implemented as domestic GAAP in the global diffusion of IFRS adoption, indicating the probable presence of translational implementation.

Empirical evidence regarding IFRS adoption

Most recent accounting studies empirically analyze the economic effects of IFRS adoption (Armstrong et al., 2010; Barth, Landsman, & Lang, 2008; Daske et al., 2008; Hail & Leuz, 2007; Leuz, 2010; Li, 2010), and several review articles summarize these studies (Ahmed et al., 2013; Brüggemann, Hitz, & Sellhorn, 2013; De George, Li, & Shivakumar, 2016; Hail, Leuz, & Wysocki, 2010; ICAEW, 2014; Leuz & Wysocki, 2016; Pope & McLeay, 2011; Soderstrom & Sun, 2007; Sunder, 2011; Suzuki, 2012). In this discussion, we focus on three studies, those of Pope and McLeay (2011), who review the European IFRS experiment; De George et al. (2016), who review studies of IFRS adoption published in top journals; and Leuz and Wysocki

(2016), who review the empirical literature on the economic consequences of disclosure and financial reporting regulations.

Pope and McLeay (2011) provide insights into the development of the EU's harmonization project, the costs and benefits of IFRS adoption in Europe, and the research challenges that arise. In particular, their review of the empirical literature suggests that "the relations between market outcomes, accounting outcomes and the financial reporting regime are potentially complex" (Pope & McLeay, 2011, p. 242). Thus, they find that "results on the consequences of IFRS adoption and the quality of implementation are far from uniform across Europe, and depend on factors reflecting preparer incentives and the effectiveness of local enforcement" (Pope & McLeay, 2011, abstract).

De George et al. (2016) review the literature on the effects of IFRS adoption, but they only consider studies published in the top five journals (i.e., *Contemporary Accounting Research, Journal of Accounting and Economics, Journal of Accounting Research, Review of Accounting Studies,* and *the Accounting Review*). They show that early studies based on voluntary IFRS adopters suggest that IFRS brought (1) improved transparency, (2) a lower cost of capital, (3) improved cross-country investments, (4) better comparability of financial reports, and (5) an increased following by foreign analysts to adopting firms and countries (De George et al., 2016, abstract). However, these benefits tended to vary significantly across firms and countries. Moreover, they find that studies of mandatory IFRS adopters report "at best mixed evidence that adoption improved the quality of accounting reports" (De George et al., 2016, p. 994).

Leuz and Wysocki (2016) review empirical studies on the economic consequences of disclosure and financial reporting regulations and summarize their findings as follows: (1) Evidence of the causal effects of disclosure and financial reporting regulations is often difficult to obtain and is still relatively rare. (2) Evidence of the market-wide effects of regulation is scare, especially with regard to externalities. (3) The empirical literature heavily focuses on disclosure regulations in the US. (4) In contrast to the work on disclosure regulations, a large literature considers the effects of reporting standards internationally. (5) Researchers likely need help from legislators and regulators to make significant progress on causal estimates of regulatory effects and cost-benefit analyses (Leuz & Wysocki, 2016, pp. 529–531). Specifically, they note the cross-sectional heterogeneity in economic consequences and the difficulty obtaining convergence of accounting practices among jurisdictions and firms that adopt IFRS.

A pervasive finding in studies on mandatory IFRS adoption is that the results exhibit considerable cross-sectional heterogeneity. That is, the observed economic outcomes around IFRS adoption vary greatly across countries, institutional regimes, and firms. [. . .] As such, the IFRS literature largely confirms that adopting a single set of reporting *standards* is not sufficient to obtain convergence in reporting *practices*.

(Leuz & Wysocki, 2016, p. 591, *italics* original)

To explain this heterogeneity and difficulty, Leuz and Wysocki (2016) point out that "there are important interactions and complementarities between reporting systems and various institutional factors" (p. 530).

In summary, the prior literature shows that IFRS adoption has significant positive effects on financial reporting and capital markets, such as increases in the quality and comparability of financial reporting, to some extent, but these consequences are non-uniform across countries, jurisdictions, and firms because they are affected by certain institutional factors and incentives for IFRS adoption (mandatory or voluntary). As such, the interactions and complementarities between accounting systems and other institutional factors suggest "major opportunities for future research" (Leuz & Wysocki, 2016, pp. 530–531)

Strategic response to IFRS

Relatively few studies in international journals focus on jurisdictions' responses to institutional pressure for IFRS implementation. For instance, Albu et al. (2014) draw on institutional theory to investigate the translation and application of IFRS in the local context of Romania, and they examine how companies based in a country with code-law institutional logic translate IFRS into accounting practice. In particular, using Oliver's (1991) strategic framework of acquiescence, compromise, avoidance, defiance, and manipulation, they find that the relationships among the regulator, professional bodies, and auditors is specific to the local context. Thus, stakeholders have a variety of strategic responses toward the pressure to adopt IFRS, and, moreover, the interests of these constituents have changed over time.

Ramanna (2013, 2015) investigates the effect of fundamental differences in international political dynamics on jurisdictions' responses to IFRS, with a particular focus on Canada, China, and India. In so doing, Ramanna (2013) develops a framework to characterize the international political dynamics of the globalization of accounting standards. This framework is represented by a two-dimensional matrix, where one dimension represents the jurisdiction's proximity to existing political power at the IASB, and the other dimension represents its potential political power at the IASB. Within this framework, Japan has lower existing political power and higher potential power, and he suggests that Japan follows the future strategies of "align IFRS with self" and "develop carve-outs."

Although Yonekura, Gallhofer, and Haslam (2012) do not directly examine IFRS adoption in Japan, they provide many implications from a historical perspective. They investigate the Japanese government's response to external and internal pressures related to bilateral trade negotiations with the US between 1989 and 2008, and they reveal both outside and inside pressures or tensions as part of the negotiations.

> External pressure to ostensibly converge corporate governance (including accounting) systems and practices has promoted Anglo-American ways that differ from established Japanese ways. At the same time there has been a field of tension within Japan so that some constituencies have sought to effectively embrace neo-liberalism, at least in a Japanese way, whilst others have sought to resist or counter the external pressures. Some pressures to change have given rise to few problems being relatively non-controversial and securing ready acceptance in Japan.
>
> (p. 328)

Moreover, their study argues that the controversy or tension around IFRS adoption in Japan is one of the most important future research areas. However, based on their analysis, they reach the following conclude:

> [T]here is a clear sense that pressures to converge accounting are not at this stage deemed especially threatening to influential groups in Japan; things are already managed in terms of Japanese ways and this respect a Japanese form of 'convergence' has been underway. From the beginning of the bilateral trade negotiations in 1989, rapid developments in corporate governance took place in terms of transparency and accounting disclosure, i.e. 'convergence' towards IAS/IFRS. There has ostensibly been support for this type of change by powerful interest groups within Japan as well as outside of Japan. Inside pressure (*naiatsu*) as well as outside pressure (*gaiatsu*) both were at work in facilitating change in the area of accounting disclosure.
>
> (p. 328)

Matsubara and Endo (2018) focus on the efforts of the ASBJ, a private-sector standard-setting body, to reconcile the pressure to adopt IFRS with Japanese GAAP by translating IFRS to the local context. They show that the ASBJ faces four categories of competing pressures or discourses from various stakeholders – mutual authentication, modification, carve-out, and active acceptance – and that the ASBJ translated this pressure in three ways: modification (i.e., modifying Japanese GAAP), optional adoption (i.e., allowing voluntary IFRS adoption), and new standards (i.e., developing JMIS).

Prior studies of Japan

Although accounting regulations in Japan represent a unique case of evolutionary diversity, few prior studies have examined the reason for this phenomenon and its theoretical implications in depth, especially in international journals. We summarize the existing literature in the following discussion.

First, Tsujiyama (2014) summarizes the basic consensus regarding the discussion of IFRS adoption in Japan over time as follows. (1) IFRS is a set of high-quality accounting standards, and financial statements conforming to IFRS are transparent, and, thus, the global adoption of IFRS increases the comparability of financial statements (from the establishment of the IASB in 2001 to the Tokyo Agreement in 2007). (2) If the US adopts IFRS, Japan will be isolated in the global accounting arena unless it also adopts IFRS (around 2009, when the BAC issued the *Interim Report*). (3) Japan's influence in the IASB/IFRS Foundation will be reduced unless it adopts IFRS (around 2013, when the BAC issued the *Present Policy*) (p. 37). External factors, such as the pressures from and stances of the EU, the US, and the IASB/IFRS Foundation, were always part of the background for these discussions (Hiramatsu, 2015). At the same time, as Yonekura et al. (2012) suggest, regulatory authorities in Japan may have taken advantage of these pressures to carry out their own policies. For instance, Usui (2015) suggests that "the BAC and other regulatory authorities (e.g. the Ministry of Finance in Japan) often use the rhetoric of 'internationalization' in regulatory reforms" (p. 343, footnote 14).

In addition, Tokuga (2015) and Tsujiyama (2015) consider the more inherent or theoretical challenges to IFRS adoption in Japan. Tokuga (2015) suggests that the three most basic differences between Japanese GAAP and IFRS are the prioritization of net income, the treatment of the recycling option (to recycle fair value changes in OCI to profit and loss), and the amortization of goodwill. Moreover, Tokuga (2015) reports that preparers in Japan find implementing and interpreting of the principles-based accounting standards of IFRS difficult, which present a practical challenge. Tsujiyama (2015) also indicates that "the theoretical contradiction within IFRS" (Tsujiyama, 2015, p. 3), rather than institutional factors, such as interactions and complementarities between accounting standards and other institutions or standard-setting by private sector bodies, is the most significant obstacle to IFRS becoming a uniform standard worldwide. Here, the theoretical contradictions within IFRS refer to discrepancies between the ideal accounting model that was first presented by the newly-born IASB and the expectations of market participants.

Tsunogaya (2016) focuses on the BAC, a public-sector standard-setting body, and identifies issues important to BAC members based on their opinions regarding mandatory IFRS adoption in Japan using a content analysis. By analyzing related BAC meetings, Tsunogaya (2016) shows that representatives from accounting academics, the manufacturing industry, and the FSA (i.e., opponents) indicated a higher level of disapproval toward the mandatory adoption of IFRS than do representatives from the Japanese Institute of Certified Public Accountants (JICPA) (i.e., proponents) (p. 829). Tsunogaya also suggests that opponents tend to consider the local context (or institutional complementarities between domestic systems) and to recommend a cautious convergence approach (i.e., voluntary IFRS adoption), whereas proponents tend to emphasize the global context (i.e., the international comparability of financial reporting and the attractiveness of Japanese capital markets) and to support a direct adoption approach (i.e., mandatory IFRS adoption). Moreover, Tsunogaya and Tokuga (2015) suggest that "most Japanese constituents prefer a cautious approach . . . to a direct approach" (p. 327).

Sanada (2018) aims to understand the impact of the global harmonization of accounting standards and the institutional change from public to private sector standard-setting bodies on the legal backing of accounting standards, and, thus, examines the unique coexistence of four sets of accounting standards in Japan through this lens. The study confirms that four accounting standards are commonly formalized into the domestic legal system through *ex post* public sector endorsements, although the standard-setting processes and public delegations can differ. Japan is an interesting example of hybridization between legally incomplete *ex ante* delegation to the private sector standard-setting bodies and *ex post* endorsement by the public sector; in other words, Japan allows a hybrid of "statutory control" and "professional control" (p. 339). Moreover, the study suggests that "the change in the legalization of ASBJ standards has taken place in the context of the voluntary adoption of IFRS and this change, paradoxically, suggests the need to strengthen the role of the state" (p. 340).

Summary

Prior reviews of international accounting studies suggest a significant increase in the number of studies that use empirical research methodologies. Such studies show that, on one hand, the adoption of IFRS brought significant benefits to adopting firms and countries (e.g.improved transparency, a lower cost of capital, improved cross-country investments, better comparability of financial reports, and an increased following by foreign analysis). On the other hand, these benefits tended to vary significantly across firms and countries owing to institutional and cultural factors. Moreover, case studies of specific countries the existence of moderating factors for IFRS adoption effects, such as legal origins, enforcement, the conformity between IFRS and domestic GAAP, incentives for adoption, and the difference in the models employed. Furthermore, pure IFRS are not always used as domestic GAAP in adopting countries.

Furthermore, prior literature on IFRS adoption in Japan highlights the theoretical contradiction between Japanese GAAP and IFRS as well as the importance of institutional factors. These studies also suggest that both inside and outside pressures facilitated the accounting change in Japan and that different stakeholder groups offered a variety of opinions and arguments.

Based on this literature review, we seek to carry out our investigation by considering the institutional effects on IFRS adoption in Japan, theoretical contradictions between Japanese GAAP and IFRS, and the diversity of opinions and their changes over time.

Theoretical background

Drawing from regulation theory, we reconstruct the following three basic categories for our study's theoretical framework: public interest theory, capture theory, and cultural theory (or alternative approach).

Theoretical frame of regulation theory

On one hand, the GAAP chosen by preparers are broadly an issue of accounting choice or accounting policy. On the other hand, the GAAP adopted jurisdictions adopt as financial reporting rules or "broader policy issues in standard setting" (Kothari, Ramanna, & Skinner, 2010, p. 263) are an issue of accounting regulations. In other words, accounting regulations incorporate disclosure and reporting regulations more broadly. Leuz and Wysocki (2016) present a broad definition of these regulations as "a central authority formally creating and interpreting disclosure and reporting rules, monitoring compliance with these rules, and enforcing and imposing penalties for deviations from the rules" (p. 527). We follow this definition in this analysis.

Although accounting regulations have been discussed as a political process (Watts & Zimmerman, 1986), some recent studies review the theoretical background for accounting regulations (Baudot, 2014; Baudot & Walton, 2014; Cooper & Robson, 2006; Kothari, Ramanna, & Skinner, 2010; Richardson & Kilfoyle, 2009). Drawing from Richardson and Kilfoyle's (2009) theoretical framework (i.e., public interest theory, capture theory, corporatist theory, negotiate order theory, and cultural theory), we reconstruct three basic categories of regulation theory: public interest theory, capture theory, and cultural (or alternative) theory (see Table 1.1).

Public interest theory

The public interest theory of regulation, based on political economy, describes the necessity of regulation. This theory describes regulation as "a benevolent and socially efficient response to market failure" (Kothari et al., 2010, p. 269) and, thus, justifies state intervention.[2] Under this theory, regulations "protect and benefit society as a whole" (*ibid*, p. 270), and the regulatory authority (e.g. the accounting standard setter) is presumed to be "a neutral intermediary representing the public interest" (Baudot, 2014, p. 218).

Under the law, the term "balancing" (Aleinikoff, 1987; Giner, 2018; Tudor, 2013) is generally used as a metaphor to describe a coordinated approach to various conflicts.

> In almost all conflicts, especially those that make their way into a legal system, there is something to be said in favor of two or more outcomes. Whatever result is chosen, someone will be advantaged and someone will be disadvantaged; some policy will be promoted at the expense of some other. Hence it is often said that a "balancing operation" must be undertaken, with the "correct" decision seen as the one yielding the greatest net benefit.
>
> (Aleinikoff, 1987, p. 943)

Thus, this term can be used to describe a "conflict between public interest and private interest" (Tudor, 2013) or "to explain the public interest by breaking rules to rescue the country or the industry" (Giner, 2018).

Capture theory

Like the public-interest theory, capture theory is based on political economy. This theory, however, is based on the notion of "regulatory failure" rather than that of "market failure." Thus, capture theory assumes that regulation is "an economic good subject to the forces of supply and demand" (Richardson & Kilfoyle, 2009, p. 320), and that regulation results from a self-serving use of the political process or rent-seeking actions by various stakeholders. This theory evolved into two variations: economics of regulation theory and the ideology theory of regulation. The former variation assumes that the regulatory body consists of self-interested individuals

Table 1.1 Theories of regulation

Theory	Explanation	References
Public interest theory	Regulation is the means by which the state intervenes to overcome market failures	Pigou (1932); Coase (1937); Williamson (1985)
Capture theory	Regulation is the result of a self-serving use of the political process	Bernstein (1955)
Economics of regulation theory	Regulation is supplied by regulators in response to the demand for regulation by various interest groups	Stigler (1971); Posner (1974); Peltzman (1976)
Ideology theory	Interest groups lobby regulators in order to convey their specific knowledge and/or ideological brief about the issues being regulated	Watts and Zimmerman (1978); Ramanna (2015)
Cultural theory		
Corporatist theory	The state delegates its regulatory authority to private sector bodies in return for their control of the regulated population	Richardson (1989); Mattli and Büthe (2005); Büthe and Mattli (2011)
Negotiated order theory	Regulation as a negotiated order develops through the complex interplay of various factors	Hopwood (1987); Robson (1991)
Cultural theory	Regulation is concerned with the interplay between institutions based on common values and/or social norms	Harrison and McKinnon (1986); Merino and Mayper (2001)

Source: Authors, referring to Baudot (2014), Kothari et al. (2010), Richardson and Kilfoyle (2009).

who supply regulation in response to demand from various interest groups. Thus, "regulation is less about the public interest than about competition for power between different interest groups, who in turn have the power to influence outcomes" (Baudot, 2014, p. 219). The latter variation presumes that interest groups lobby regulators to convey their specific knowledge or ideological understanding about the objects of regulations.

Cultural theory

The above two theories address the necessity and problems of regulation from an economic perspective. In contrast, cultural theory discusses "accounting regulation in its organizational and social context" (Cooper & Robson, 2006, p. 428). Thus, this is also called the alternative approach, but we refer to it here as cultural theory in a broad sense.[3] This theory has three variations: corporatist theory, negotiated order theory, and cultural theory (in a narrow sense). Corporatist theory suggests that "the state enters into a bargain with private sector bodies providing them with access to state power and resources in return for their control of the regulated population" (Richardson & Kilfoyle, 2009, p. 320). Negotiated order theory focuses more on process and, thus, addresses the question of "how regulation is created and implemented rather than why regulation is created" (Richardson & Kilfoyle, 2009, p. 320, italic in original). This theory treats regulation as a negotiated order developed through the complex interplay of various factors. In contrast, cultural theory places more emphasis on the role of culture or social values. Thus, implicit regulation appears "through social norms monitored and enforced informally by market participants" (Richardson & Kilfoyle, 2009, p. 330), whereas explicit regulation is established under the law and formally organized with enforcement.

Methodology

This study aims to construct a historical narrative of the interplay between accounting standards in Japan and theories of regulation. For that purpose, we examine the causal process that resulted in the coexistence of four sets of accounting standards in Japan, and we attempt to provide minimally sufficient explanations for this unique coexistence through the lens of the theories of regulation.

Empirical frames

Richardson and Kilfoyle (2009, p. 312) also suggest that the historical study of accounting regulation has typically followed one of five empirical strategies:

1   Providing a simple cross-sectional description of regulation,
2   Exploring possible causes and consequences of regulatory events,
3   Identifying 'exogenous shocks' and looking for the impact of those events on continuing regulations and regulatory process,
4   Looking for regulatory changes and examining the motives and implication of the change, or
5   Comparing cases or periods with variation in specific factors (or rival causes) thought to affect accounting regulation.

This study essentially follows strategies 2, 3, and 4 in examining the causal process that resulted in the coexistence of four sets of accounting standards in Japan. To achieve this task, we use the process-tracing method as our overall analytical strategy.

Process tracing

Process tracing is "the examination of intermediate steps in a process to make inferences about hypotheses on how that process took place and whether and how it generated the outcome of interest" (Bennett & Checkel, 2015, p. 6). This approach attempts to trace the links between possible causes and observed outcomes using "histories, archival documents, interview transcripts, and other sources to see whether the causal process a theory hypothesizes or implies in a case is in fact evident in the sequence and values of the intervening variables in that case" (George & Bennett, 2005, p. 6). Process tracing has three basic variants: theory testing, theory building, and explaining outcome. This study uses the explaining-outcome process-tracing approach to craft "a minimally sufficient explanation of a particular outcome, with sufficiency defined as an explanation that accounts for all of the important aspects of an outcome with no redundant parts being present" (Beach & Pedersen, 2016, p. 18).

A special feature of causal inference in process tracing is "abduction," in which event observation and hypothesis development occur simultaneously.[4] The explaining-outcome process-tracing approach tests a working hypothesis, which is constructed inductively based on theories from prior studies (theories of regulation, in this study), in a factual investigation and, then, successively modifies the hypothesis to construct a minimally sufficient explanation.[5] This approach has advantages over inductive or deductive inference because it can explain both equifinality, in which various causes create the same result, and multifinality, in which the same cause can lead to different outcomes.[6]

Research setting

This historical case study of accounting regulations in Japan focuses on the period from 2001, when the ASBJ was established, to 2015, when the ASBJ issued JMIS. To investigate the causal mechanism that resulted in the unique coexistence of four sets of consolidated accounting standards in Japan, this study uses a process-tracing approach. This methodology combines a narrative that inductively analyzes historical events and a theoretical approach that deductively analyzes Japan's unique regulatory setting based on an existing framework of regulation theory. Thus, this study consists of two steps. In the first step, we construct a historical narrative using publicly available sources (in Chapter II), and, in the second step, we analyze the theoretical implications of Japan's current situation in through the lens of regulation theory (in Chapter III).

Data and analysis

This study relies on publicly available documentation, such as official reports, discussion documents and related responses, and a range of additional information (i.e. all of the documents listed in "Primary sources"). We select and collect these documents from the ASBJ web page and other resources.

Process tracing is our overall analytical strategy. However, this strategy combines two analytical strategies. First, to reconstruct the historical narrative of accounting regulation in Japan, we perform a contextual and interpretive analysis of documents that we collected. Moreover, in our theoretical analysis, we use a pattern-matching technique (Langley, 1999; Reay & Jones, 2016; Yin, 2018) inspired by the theoretical framework of Allison and Zelikow (1999), who uses three conceptual models, rational actor, organizational behavior, and governmental politics models to explain the decision-making process of the US government during the Cuban missile crisis.

A pattern-matching technique compares data (or a pattern identified from an empirical investigation) with ideal types[7] and then "evaluate(s) their data to determine how well it matches with the ideal type" (Reay & Jones, 2016, p. 446). The advantage of this technique is "the analyst proposes several alternative interpretations of the same events based on different but internally coherent sets of a priori theoretical premises. He or she then assesses the extent to which each theoretical template contributes to a satisfactory explanation" (Langley, 1999, p. 698). Thus, we compare our findings with the three categories of regulation theory described above (e.g. public interest, capture, and cultural) and seek to propose several alternative interpretations of the evolution of accounting regulations in Japan.

Notes

1 They define IAR as research focusing on (1) accounting phenomena in one country that provide lessons or repercussions extending for other countries, (2) accounting phenomena related to multinational enterprises, and (3) global movements shaping the direction of accounting and comparative accounting requirements and practices (Baker & Barbu, 2007, p. 273, citing Wallace & Meek, 2002). On the contrary, they define IAH research as a subset of financial accounting research and IAR that investigates "the arguments for efforts made towards, and trends in the direction of achieving international harmonization to financial standards" (Baker & Barbu, 2007, p. 274).
2 Public interest theory addresses four commonly offered justifications for market failures: (1) natural monopoly, (2) externalities, (3) information asymmetries, and (4) excess competitions (Kothari et al., 2010, p. 269, citing Breyer, 1982).

3 We refer to "cultural theory" in contrast with the two economic-based theories as a matter of convenience. Thus, as used in this volume, this term is conceptually different from the cultural theories based on Hofstede's framework (e.g. Gray, 1988) and the Douglasian framework (e.g. Linsley & Shrives, 2014). Instead, it refers more broadly to "a common standard or ideal of social organization" (Scott, 1931, p. 3).

4 Abduction takes the following form of inference (Peirce, 1955, p. 151): (1) A surprising fact, C, is observed. (2) However, if A were true, C would be a matter of course. Hence, (3) there is reason to suspect that A is true.

5 Thus, our aim is not to "build or test more general theories but to craft a (minimally) sufficient explanation of the outcome of the case where the ambitions are more case-centric than theory-oriented" (Beach & Pedersen, 2013, p. 3).

6 We ontologically rely upon realism, but our epistemological stance is not positivism but rather "critical realism" (Bryman, 2016), which investigates an underlying structure (or causal mechanism) rather than a simple phenomenon (or causal relationship). In that sense, this study falls between realism and constructionism.

7 Reay and Jones (2016, p. 447), citing Thornton, Ocasio, and Lounsbury (2012), suggest that ideal types do not represent the social reality but instead function as "tool(s) to interpret cultural meaning" and "help the researchers avoid getting bogged down in merely reproducing the often-confusing empirical situation" (Thornton et al., 2012, p. 52).

2 Accounting regulation in Japan

Institutional background

For the sake of convenience, especially for international readers, we review the development of accounting regulations in Japan before 2000 and illustrate its special features in this section.

Japan before 2001

After the post-war reconstruction period (1945–1955) and the high economic growth period (1955–1970), the Nixon shock (or dollar shock) of 1971 and the oil crisis of 1973 kicked off Japan's economic development in the era of low growth.[1] However, in this time period, the so-called Japanese economic system (or management system) also enjoyed further success before encountering dysfunction. Noguchi (1998) calls this system "the 1940 system," which was originally designed to fight against the Allied Forces and identifies the basic elements of the system as follows: (1) the employment practices, such as lifetime employment, the seniority wage, and in-house labor unions, that are typically observed in large organizations; (2) the weak influence of shareholders on corporate decisions; (3) an indirect financial system; (4) intensive government interventions in private economic activities, including, in particular, the protection of low-productivity sectors, such as agriculture and small businesses; (5) a tax structure that relies heavily on income tax; and (6) a government structure in which local governments are strictly controlled by the central government (p. 404).

This system worked very efficiently in the 1970s and 1980s, and Japan especially enjoyed an economic bubble in the late 1980s. However, after the asset price bubble burst in early 1992, the Japanese economy declined for more than a decade. In this period, the once-admired Japanese economic system became an obstacle. Noguchi (1998) suggests that this system became obsolete for the following two reasons:

> First, it is difficult for workers to move from one company to another under the lifetime employment and seniority wage system. This works as an obstacle to changing the industrial structure. Second, under the indirect financial system, it is difficult to supply investment funding for venture businesses whose futures are uncertain. Although several attempts have been made to finance venture businesses, only insufficient funds have been provided for them.
>
> (Noguchi, 1998, p. 407)

In this context, structural reforms of Japan's economic system became an urgent issue, and, thus, the restructuring of Japan's accounting regulations was also under the spotlight.[2]

Triangular system

From the late 1940s until the enactment of the Company Act (2005), which took effect on May 2006, the so-called triangular three-code legal system, which consisted of the Commercial Code, the Securities and Exchange Law (SEL), and the Corporate Income Tax Law (CITL), constituted "a fairly detailed statutory foundation for disclosure under Japanese generally accepted accounting principles (GAAP)" (Benston, Bromwich, Litan, & Wagenhofer, 2006, p. 167). The objectives of financial statements prepared in accordance with each of these laws differ. For instance, as Cooke and Kikuya (1992) explain:

> The underlying objective of financial statements prepared in accordance with Commercial Code requirements is to protect creditors and current investors. Thus, emphasis is placed on disclosures which provide information on the valuation of assets for solvency purposes, availability of earnings for dividend distributions, and on creditworthiness and earning power.
>
> (p. 173)

> The main objective of reporting under the Securities and Exchange Law is adequate and appropriate disclosure on the results and financial position of the company for the protection of general investors.
>
> (p. 174)[3]

Additionally, the main objective of the CITL is to ensure the appropriate implementation of taxation. Despite these differences, the three ways of calculating incomes in the triangular system, that is, the accounting profit calculated under the SEL, the profit available for dividend calculated under the Commercial Code, and the taxable income calculated under the CITL, are nearly equal, whereas, in the US and the UK, these accounting numbers are different in principle.

Japanese GAAP before 2000

Under the triangular system, Japanese GAAP consisted of basic principles (i.e. Business Accounting Principles) and accounting standards (i.e. Opinions) issued by the Business Accounting Deliberation Council (BADC)[4] as well as interpretation and implementation guidance issued by JICPA, and "must be consistent with three laws and cannot override them" (Benston et al., 2006, p. 167). Until recently, the Business Accounting Principles were the main pillar of Japanese GAAP.

The Business Accounting Principles were originally issued as the *Working Rules for Preparing Financial Statements* by the Investigation Committee on Business Accounting Systems (ICBAS) of the Economic Stabilization Board, a former body of the BADC, on July 6, 1949. They were one of the measures for rebuilding the post-war economy under American occupation, and, thus, "there was considerable US influence over these accounting statements" (Cooke & Kikuya, 1992, p. 97). The calculation structure in the Business Accounting Principles was significant in that it showed "the calculation norm based on a certain accounting perspective" (Tsumori, 2002, p. 330). In other words, the Business Accounting Principles suggested a shift away from a balance sheet-based model (or balance sheet-oriented accounting thought), which was once embodied by *Working Rules for Financial Statements* issued by the Ministry of Commerce and Industry of the Empire of Japan in 1934, and a shift toward an income statement-based model (or income statement-oriented accounting thought), which became dominant in the US starting in the 1930s.

Consolidated accounting system in Japan

In Japan, traditional accounting disclosures, based on the Commercial Code, are "prepared for a single year only and on an individual company basis" (Cooke & Kikuya, 1992, p. 173). However, the consolidated accounting system was introduced in Japan based on *Opinion on the Establishment of the System of Consolidated Financial Statements*, released by the BADC in June 1975, and *Ordinance on Terminology, Forms, and Preparation Methods of Consolidated Financial Statements* (Ordinance of the Ministry of Finance No. 28 of 1976), released in October 1976. At this time, 39 representative Japanese firms had already registered with the SEC and had been preparing their consolidated financial statements under US GAAP. Thus, as an extraordinary measure under Paragraph 2 of the Supplementary Provisions of the Ordinance, these companies were permitted to use US GAAP in Japan as well.

Accounting big bang and the establishment of the ASBJ

Although Japan experienced apparent success in terms of economic, financial, and political stability in the 1980s, after the sudden collapse of the asset price bubble, it faced economic, financial, and political distress for more than a decade. The main reason for this prolonged economic slump was that the old Japanese economic system (or the 1940 system) became dysfunctional in a new environment in which the world was becoming more globalized.[5] Thus, "Japan needed to adapt its economic and political institutions to a new environment" (Cargill & Sakamoto, 2008, p. 3). In this context, the Japanese government launched Japan's version of the "financial big bang" to deregulate and liberalize the financial sector in 1996.[6]

> [I]t envisaged a major redesign of Japan's financial system and was based on three principles: (1) to establish free, open, and competitive markets; (2) to ensure fair financial practices through transparent and enforced regulation and supervision; and (3) to initiate accounting, legal, and regulatory institutional reforms to make Japan's financial system internationally compatible.
>
> (Cargill & Sakamoto, 2008, p. 110)

Apparent external pressure from the US under the *US.-Japan Enhanced Initiative on Deregulation and Competition Policy* (Enhanced Initiative) between the Hashimoto Cabinet and the Clinton Administration from 1997 to 2001 was behind this launch.[7] In the Enhanced Initiative, the US urged the Japanese government to undertake measures to "'address reform of relevant government laws, regulations, and guidance which have the effect of substantially impeding market access for competitive goods and services in order to enhance consumers' interests and to increase efficiency and promote economic activity" (MOFA, 1997). In addition, a criticism of "wonderland accounting" (Financial Times, 1997) claimed that Japanese accounting and audit practices were untrustworthy.[8] Thus, restoring confidence in the Japanese accounting system was an urgent task.

Along with this reformation and in response to the pressure to harmonize Japanese GAAP with international accounting standards (i.e. US GAAP and IAS/IFRS), a series of accounting reforms, called the accounting big bang, were carried out, and Japanese accounting standards were considerably revised. These revisions addressed accounting standards for consolidated financial statements, retirement benefits, tax effect accounting, financial instruments, the impairment of assets, and business combinations (Koga & Rimmel, 2007, p. 223). This reform mainly featured a shift in emphasis from individual to consolidated accounting[9] and the harmonization of international accounting standards and Japanese GAAP. Table 2.1 describes the accounting standards issued as part of the accounting big bang).

In addition, the Financial Accounting Standards Foundation (FASF), the private-sector founding body of the ASBJ, was created by the founders of ten representative economic organizations in Japan in July 2001. Specifically, these organizations were the Japan Business Foundation (Keidanren); JICPA; the Tokyo Stock Exchanges; the Japan Securities Dealers Association; the Japanese Bankers Association; the Life Insurance Association of Japan; the Marine & Fire Insurance Association of Japan, Inc.; the Japan Chamber of Commerce & Industry; the Security Analysts Association of Japan; and the Corporate Finance Research Institute (COFRI).[10] The purpose of the FASF is "to promote progress of corporate finance disclosure

Table 2.1 Accounting opinions/standards issued in the accounting big bang

Date	Opinion/Standards	Issuer
June 1997	Opinion on the review of the consolidated financial statements system	BAC (BADC)
March 1998	Opinion on establishment of accounting standards for interim financial reporting	BAC (BADC)
March 1998	Opinion on establishment of accounting standards for cash flow statements	BAC (BADC)
March 1998	Opinion on establishment of accounting standards for research and development costs	BAC (BADC)
June 1998	Opinion on establishment of accounting standards for retirement benefits	BAC (BADC)
October 1998	Opinion on establishment of accounting standards for tax effect accounting	BAC (BADC)
January 1999	Accounting Standards for Financial Instruments	BAC (BADC)
October 1999	Opinion on revision of accounting standards for the translation of foreign currency transactions	BAC (BADC)
2002/08	Opinion on establishment of asset-impairment accounting standards	BAC (BADC)
2003/10	Opinion on issuance of accounting standards for Business Combination in Japan	BAC (BADC)
2005/12	Accounting Standards for Presentation of Net Assets in the Balance Sheet	ASBJ
2005/12	Accounting Standards for Share-based Payment	ASBJ

Source: Authors refer to Miyauchi and Tokuga (2007), Table 1, p. 262.

and soundness of the capital markets in Japan by developing generally accepted accounting standards" (Keidanren et al., 2001), and it is managed by the board of directors and the trustees as well as the Financial Accounting Foundation in the US and the International Accounting Standards Committee (IASC) Foundation (now the IFRS Foundation). As an independent body, the FASF is funded through a membership system to encourage participation by a wide range of interested parties, such as preparers and users of financial statements, auditors, academics, and so on.

The organizational structure of the ASBJ, which was promptly established by the FASF, is the same as that of the US Financial Accounting Standards Board (FASB) and the IASB, and consists of board members, technical committees, working groups, and a secretariat.

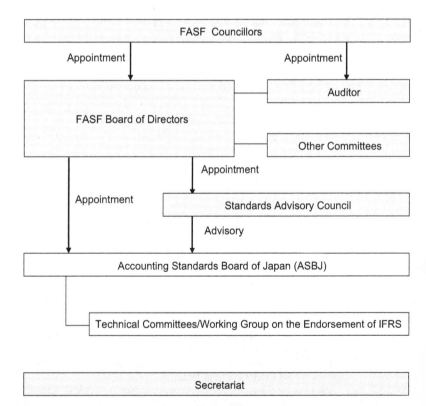

Figure 2.1 Organizational structure of the FASF/ASBJ

Source: ASBJ/FASF web page. www.asb.or.jp/en/fasf-asbj/organization.html

The ASBJ developed its accounting standards following the due process established by its administration rules. However, the FASF set up *Rules on the Due Process for the Development of Japanese GAAP and Japan's Modified International Standards* (Due Process Rules) in June 2013, and, thus, the ASBJ developed its accounting standards in accordance with these rules.[11] After that, the ASBJ took over the authority for setting accounting standards from the BADC, which was an advisory body of the FSA, a successor of Ministry of Finance. This transfer of authority over accounting standards from the public to the private sector has been favorably evaluated as "a 180-degrees conversion" (Endo, Komiyama, Sakase, Tagaya, & Hashimoto, 2015, p. 457). However, it can also be seen as only "a functional transfer" (Chiba, 2012, p. 477) because the BADC, as an advisory body, had rather little authority relative to, for example, the US Securities and Exchange Commission (SEC).

The immediate cause of this privatization was to appeal to principal countries, such as Germany, to allow Japan to participate in the newly restructured IASB. Japanese policymakers believed that "a private sector body was a condition for a seat" (Sanada, 2018, p. 353) on the board. At the same time, Saito, the first chairman of the ASBJ, suggested that "Japan had finished the postwar accounting reform that pursued the US model under the government initiative, and reached the stage where financial market participants should bear responsibility for making the market system by themselves" (Saito, 2014, pp. 240–241). More importantly, however, Japan needed to resolve "the legend clause problem" and re-establish confidence in its accounting system. After the Asian financial crisis, the Big Five accounting firms, as defined at the time, required that Japanese companies' financial statements include a legend clause in notes or audit reports that warned that the financial statements were prepared under Japanese GAAP (Endo et al., 2015, p. 283; Kimura & Ogawa, 2007, p. 225). As this requirement implied that Japanese GAAP were regarded as low-quality accounting standards by these accounting firms and their clients, quickly improving the quality of Japanese accounting standards was an urgent matter.

The accounting big bang also facilitated changes in Japan's legal system; the Company Act and the Financial Instruments and Exchange Act (FIEA) were both enacted in 2006. In contrast with the provisions in the Commercial Code, the Company Act delegates the accounting regulation of listed and unlisted public companies to FIEA, with the exception of the calculation of the profit available for dividends. Thus, the calculation of retained earnings is relatively independent of that of accounting profits. Moreover, the relationship between the three laws has become "loosely coupled" insofar as public companies are concerned (Tokuga, 2012a, p. 123).

Legitimacy of Japanese GAAP

Regarding the normativity or legitimacy of the accounting standards set by the ASBJ, the ASBJ is only responsible for setting accounting standards and facilitating the international convergence of its standards. As mentioned above, the FSA originally possessed the authority to set accounting standards in Japan, and the FSA *ex post* endorsed ASBJ standards. In other words, the normativity of ASBJ standards is secured by this FSA endorsement. As a result, "there is no provision in administrative laws" (Chiba, 2012, p. 477), and "accounting standards themselves are provided for neither in the Company Act and [sic] the Financial Instruments and Exchange Act" (Nishikawa, 2014, p. 69). More specifically, the ASBJ standards became statutory rules only owing to a reference in the "*Tsutatsu*" (a circular notice by the FSA) under the provision of the SEL, then the FIEA. Thus, many accounting researchers in Japan underscored "the ambiguity and uncertainty of the formal authority and legal bases of the ASBJ" (Sanada, 2018, p. 347) and its standards. Later, in 2009, the "*Kinyucho-Kokuji*" (a public notice by the FSA) postulated that the "business accounting standards that are generally accepted as fair and appropriate" include those developed by the ASBJ, and thus, the ASBJ standards were legitimized in the Japanese legal system.

From a practical perspective, however, nine of the founding members of the ASBJ (excluding the COFRI) issued a statement that providing assurance of the enforceability of the ASBJ standards in May 2002.

> Business accounting standards issued by the Accounting Standards Board of Japan are generally accepted as fair and appropriate business accounting standards under fair and appropriate procedures. Therefore, these standards are expected to be accounting norms in which we founding-members, the members, and other market participants conform to and are in accordance with.
>
> (Keidanren et al., 2002)

In this way, the ASBJ standards are enforceable accounting rules in Japan in practice.

Achieving the convergence of IFRS and Japanese GAAP (2001–2006)

During this period, the ASBJ accelerated the harmonization of international accounting standards and Japanese GAAP. Thus, Japanese accounting standards were considerably revised.

Domestic and international situation

In the early 2000s, Japan faced significant challenges, such as accomplishing the accounting big bang and settling the legend clause problem. However, in the domestic political scene, Junichiro Koizumi was elected prime minister in April 2001 (his tenure ended at the end of September 2006). While Koizumi was in office, Japan experienced "significant changes in politics and the economy" (Cargill & Sakamoto, 2008, p. 17) and made some progress in fiscal reconstruction and economic recovery.

> Koizumi wanted a faster resolution of the huge nonperforming loan problem in the banking system, more drastic restructuring of "zombie" corporations and banks, and more deregulation and privatization to increase the efficiency and competitiveness of the Japanese economy. In this respect, he departed from the approach adopted by all previous LDP [Liberal Democratic Party] administrations – gradual reform while protecting and minimizing losses to client industries and sectors.
>
> (Cargill & Sakamoto, 2008, p. 18)

The most important international issue during this period was the intimate relationship between the IASB and the FASB. In October 2002, these boards announced the issuance of a memorandum of understanding (MOU) called "the Norwalk Agreement" and agreed to undertake short-term and medium- to long-term projects to eliminate a variety of differences between IFRS and US GAAP. Moreover, a revised version of the MOU issued in February 2005 assumed that the SEC's reconciliation requirement for foreign companies would be eliminated (or relaxed) and suggested that the convergence between IFRS and US GAAP be further accelerated, specifying an end date of 2008. As Camfferman and Zeff (2015) suggest, "[b]y tradition, Japan had looked to the United States for guidance on accounting principles and standards, and US GAAP, with its extensive application guidance, was generally seen as superior to IFRSs" (p. 81). This shift in the US affected Japan's convergence strategy.

In addition, the European Committee (EC) issued the International Accounting Standards (IAS) Regulation (Regulation EC, 1606/2002) in July 2002 (EC, 2002). This regulation required all publicly traded companies in EU member states to prepare their consolidated financial statements in accordance with IFRS by 2005 at the latest. At the same time, non-EU issuers whose securities were admitted to trading on an EU regulated market or who wished to publicly offer their securities in Europe would be required "to publish a prospectus including financial statements prepared on the basis of EU endorsed IAS/IFRS or on the basis of a third country's national accounting standards (third country GAAP) if these standards are equivalent to the endorsed IAS/IFRS" (CESR, 2004), as of January 2007 (this deadline was later extended to 2009). Thus, the newly formed ASBJ also had to deal with this equivalence assessment from the EC.

ASBJ's initial stance on convergence

The ASBJ essentially followed the so-called two-step market approach to harmonize Japanese GAAP with international standards. First, it sought mutual recognition by reducing the differences between Japanese GAAP and international standards (i.e. US GAAP and IFRS) as much as possible. Next, it sought a further convergence between Japanese GAAP and international standards through market competition (Saito, 2014, pp. 242–243). Following this approach, clearly demonstrated in the ASBJ's 2004 Medium-Term Management Plan, the ASBJ launched a joint project for convergence with the IASB in March 2005.[12]

Equivalence assessments by the EU

In July 2005, the Committee of European Securities Regulators (CESR) issued technical advice on the equivalence of American, Canadian, and Japanese accounting standards with IFRS to the European Committee (EC). CESR advised that these three GAAPs, "each taken as a whole" (CESR, 2005, p. 3), were equivalent to IFRS. However, CESR did identify 26 significant differences between Japanese GAAP and IFRS (see Table 2.2).

The ASBJ took a phased approach to the IASB-ASBJ convergence project, in which "differences between the accounting standards that are relatively easy to initiate discussion about are addressed first" (ASBJ, 2006b). However, after CESR issued its statement providing technical advice on the equivalence of standards (CESR, 2005), the ASBJ switched to a new, big-picture approach, in which "all of the differences between the accounting standards are addressed from an entire perspective" (ASBJ, 2006b). The IASB-ASBJ convergence project and the response to the EC's equivalence assessment are part of the same undertaking. Thus, within its big-picture approach, the ASBJ classified major differences in accounting standards into "short-term projects," which could be completed quickly, and "long-term projects," which were the remaining projects. The ASBJ further clarified in its project plan that short-term projects were scheduled to be completed by 2008 (ASBJ, 2006c).

	Canadian GAAP	Japanese GAAP	US GAAP
Disclosure A	• Share base payment (IFRS 2) – current standard • Minority interest at historical cost (IFRS 3) • Step acquisition (IFRS 3) • Employment benefits (IAS 19) • Reversal of impairment (IAS 36) • Decommissioning costs (IAS 37) • Investment property (IAS 40)	• Share base payment (IFRS 2) –future standard ED3 Japanese GAAP • Minority interest at historical cost (IFRS 3) • Step acquisition (IFRS 3) • Catastrophic provisions (IAS 11) • Non-performing loans (IAS 12 & 13), except if disclosure is already provided • Costs for assets retirement obligation (IAS 16) • Employment benefits (IAS 19) • Translation of goodwill (IAS 21) • Fair value of derivatives (IAS 32) • Reversal of impairment (IAS 36) • Decommissioning costs (IAS 37) • Investment property (IAS 40)	• Share base payment (IFRS 2) – SFAS 123R • Minority interest at historical cost (IFRS 3) • Step acquisition (IFRS 3) • Replacement's costs (IAS 16) • Employment benefits (IAS 19) • Reversal of impairment (IAS 36) • Decommissioning costs (IAS 37) • Investment property (IAS 40)
Disclosure B	• Date of exchange (IFRS 3) • Negative goodwill (IFRS 3) • Use of LIFO (IAS 2) • Impairment test – non-discounted future cash flow (IAS 36) • Agriculture (IAS 41)	• Share Based Payments (IFRS 2) – current standard • Date of exchange (IFRS 3) • Acquired R&D (IFRS 3) • Negative goodwill (IFRS 3) • Use of LIFO & cost method (IAS 2) • Uniformity of accounting policies (IAS 28) • Impairment Test – non-discounted future cash flows (IAS 36) • Capitalization of development costs (IAS 38) • Agriculture (IAS 41)	• Share Based Payments (IFRS 2) – current standard SFAS 123 • Date of exchange (IFRS 3) • Acquired R&D (IFRS 3) • Negative goodwill (IFRS 3) • Use of LIFO (IAS 2), except if disclosure is already provided • Uniformity of accounting policies (IAS 28) • Impairment Test – non-discounted future cash flows (IAS 36) • Capitalization of development costs (IAS 38) • Agriculture (IAS 41)

(Continued)

Table 2.2 (Continued)

	Canadian GAAP	Japanese GAAP	US GAAP
Supplementary statements	• Scope of consolidation (Definition of control – QSPE) (IAS 27)	• Pooling of interests (IFRS 3) • Scope of consolidation (Definition of control – QSPE) (IAS 27) • Uniformity of accounting policies (IAS 27)	• Scope of consolidation (Definition of control – QSPE) (IAS 27)
Future work (O/S)	• Financial instruments (IAS 39): possible Disclosure A	• Financial instruments (IAS 39): Disclosure A	• Financial instruments (IAS 39): possible Disclosure A
Total	14 items	26 items	19 items

Disclosure A: Additional narrative and/or quantitative disclosures augmenting the disclosures already provided pursuant to third country GAAP (e.g. explanation of the relevant transactions and events and the method of accounting; indication of assumptions, valuation methods or hypothesis used for the measurement and recognition of the transactions and events; and disclosure of fair value of assets)

Disclosure B: Quantitative indication of the impact of an event or transaction, had this event or transaction been accounted for following IAS/IFRS provisions

Supplementary statements: Pro-forma statements, prepared and presented on the basis of third country GAAP accounting principles and of the issuer's primary financial statements, but including a limited restatement for taking account of one identified aspect of IFRS requirement that is not present of not fully applied under third country GAAP

Source: CESR (2005), modified by authors.

Stance of policy makers and constituencies

In April 2003, the LDP, the ruling party, announced its intention to submit a private member's bill suspending the implementation of mark-to-market accounting for five years and accounting for the impairment of fixed assets for two years. This bill was simply intended as an emergency economic measure. However, Ishikawa (2006) points out that this political pressure reflected the policymakers' discontent with the shift in authority for setting accounting standards from the public to the private sector or its discontent with the private sector standard-setting body itself. Thus, a basic conflict arose between the proponents of the globalization of accounting standards and political and economic nationalists.

The Keidanren issued *Seeking International Collaboration on Accounting Standards* in October 2003. This recommendation stipulated that Japanese GAAP and auditing needed to re-establish confidence because "there were criticisms by some that Japanese accounting standards lagged behind those in other countries, and that accounting and auditing in Japan was unreliable" (Keidanren, 2003). Moreover, the document urged that "accounting standards in the three major capital markets – the United States, Europe, and Japan – move in a direction in which the basic principles are unified to the greatest extent possible" (Keidanren, 2003). However, as cross-country differences along a number of dimensions remained, the Keidanren supported the mutual recognition of accounting standards in Japan, the US, and Europe.

In addition, the recommendation mentioned concerns regarding the governance and procedures of the IASB. In a joint statement with the Union des Industries de la Communauté Européenne (UNICE) in April 2004, the Keidanren reiterated the need to improve the IASB's governance and the mutual recognition of accounting standards and expressed strong opposition to the "full fair value approach" (Keidanren & UNICE, 2004). Moreover, in a June 2006 policy statement, the Keidanren declared its support for the acceleration of the convergence of accounting standards and the mutual recognition of standards in Japan, the US, and Europe (Keidanren, 2006). However, it also expressed concerns regarding the isolation of Japanese accounting standards, as IFRS and US GAAP had been further converging, whereas the decision on the equivalence of Japanese GAAP, US GAAP, and Canadian standards was deferred until fiscal year 2009.

Voluntary adoption of IFRS (2007–2011)

In this period, after the Tokyo Agreement between the IASB and the ASBJ in August 2007, the BAC, an advisory body established by the FAC, launched a special initiative to advance the voluntary adoption of IFRS in Japan. The body also discussed the mandatory adoption of IFRS in Japan.

Domestic and international arenas

In the international arena, the equivalence assessment continued, and the EC finally determined that Japanese GAAP, like US GAAP, were equivalent to IFRS, "unless there is no adequate evidence of the ASBJ achieving to timetable [sic] the objectives set out in the Tokyo Agreement" (CESR, 2007). Moreover, in the US, the SEC issued a proposed roadmap to IFRS (SEC, 2008) that could lead to the use of IFRS by US issuers starting in 2014 at the earliest. Thus, the possibility that the US would adopt IFRS increased. However, owing to the global financial crisis (2007–2008) and the change in the presidency, this trend soon stagnated in the US. However, during the financial turmoil, the G20 Washington Summit on Financial Markets and the World Economy in November 2008 suggested that the key global accounting standards bodies (e.g. the IASB and the FASB) should work to enhance their governance and "to ensure consistent application and enforcement of high-quality accounting standards" (G20, 2008). In this context, after the second Constitution Review (2008–2010), the IASB conducted organizational reforms and a new system was launched.

Meanwhile, in Japan, the ruling LDP was defeated by the Democratic Party (DPJ) in the general election held in September 2009, and the DPJ held power until December 2012.

Tokyo Agreement

In August 2007, the IASB and the ASBJ released the *Agreement on Initiatives to Accelerate the Convergence of Accounting Standards* (the Tokyo Agreement). The agreement stipulated that: (1) the major differences identified in the EC's equivalence assessment were to be eliminated by the end of 2008; (2) the remaining differences were to be removed by June 30, 2011; and (3) the ASBJ and the IASB would work closely to ensure the acceptance of the international approach in Japan, particularly in the case of the accounting standards currently being developed by the IASB that were scheduled to become effective after June 30, 2011 (BAC, 2009, pp. 3–4).

Previously, the ASBJ's basis stance was "to make efforts to eliminate differences between Japanese GAAP and IFRS through standard-setting activities aimed at the convergence" (Nishikawa, 2007, p. 12). Thus, the Tokyo Agreement was a policy change by the ASBJ.

The ASBJ Revised Project Plan

In December 2007, the ASBJ issued the Revised Project Plan, which created three project categories: (1) items identified by CESR in the equivalence assessment (short-term category); (2) differences between Japanese GAAP and IFRS excluding those in the short-term category (medium-term category); and (3) items related to the MOU between the IASB and the FASB (medium- and long-term category) (see Table 2.3). In response to this plan, the EC made the final decision that Japanese GAAP would be equivalent with IFRS on the condition that the ASBJ completed the convergence activities on the timetable given by the Revised Project Plan.

Interim Report

Initially, the ASBJ took a "cautious convergence approach" (Tsunogaya and Tokuga, 2015). However, the Tokyo Agreement with the IASB and the ASBJ in August 2007 changed the atmosphere, and the situation further shifted to a remarkable degree when the BAC (renamed from the BADC in English in 2009) approved its *Opinion on the Application of International Financial Reporting Standards (IFRS) in Japan (Interim Report)* (BAC, 2009) on June 30, 2009. At the same time, the FSA published thirteen related documents, including: (1) a proposal for the revision of the Ordinance on Terminology, Forms, and Preparation Methods of Consolidated Financial Statements; (2) a proposal for the revision of the Guidelines for the Ordinance on Terminology, Forms, and Preparation Methods of Financial Statements; and (3) a *Kinyucho-Kokuji* proposal (Public Notice by the FSA).[13]

As a special provision for application, the Ordinance stipulates that companies that meet certain requirements, referred to as "Specific Companies,"[14] can use the Designated International Accounting Standards in their consolidated financial statements. Furthermore, the *Kinyucho-Kokuji* specifies that the Designated International Accounting Standards are those developed by the IASB. In other words, the Ordinance allows individual Japanese companies to start voluntarily using IFRS for their consolidated financial statements starting with the fiscal year ending on March 31, 2010. Moreover, the Ordinance maintains the continuous application of US GAAP through fiscal year 2015 as a transitional measure.

In addition, the Interim Report indicated that the BAC would determine whether it could mandate the use of IFRS for Japanese companies by 2012 (the mandatory use of IFRS would have started in 2015 at the earliest). Furthermore, the Interim Report listed four perspectives that needed to be considered for the mandatory application of IFRS: (1) the improvement of the

Table 2.3 ASBJ Project Plan (December 2007)

Project Categories	Project Items	Target Date
1 Items advised by CESR for EU equivalence assessment purpose (short-term)	Business combinations (pooling-of-interest method and others) Inventories (LIFO) Uniformity of accounting policies (associates) Impairments of fixed assets Intangibles (R&D) Construction contracts Asset retirement obligations Retirement benefits Disclosure of FV information of financial instruments Investment property	End of 2008
2 Items remaining differences between Japanese GAAP and IFRSs except above (medium-term)	Segment reporting Business combinations (ammonization of goodwill and others) Retrospective restatement (change in accounting policy, depreciation method, and discontinued operations)	June 2011
3 Items related MOU between the IASB and the FASB (medium- and long-term)	Scope of consolidations Financial statement presentation Revenue recognition Liabilities and equity distinctions Financial instruments	At the time of implementation of new standards (expects after the date to June 2011)

Source: Release of Project Plan – Initiatives toward international convergence of accounting standards based on the Tokyo Agreement (ASBJ, 2007b), modified by authors.

international comparability of financial statements and the attractiveness of Japan's financial and capital markets to international investors, (2) the greater ease with which foreign investors could understand and analyze financial statements prepared by Japanese companies, (3) the enhancement of Japanese companies' international competitiveness, and (4) its contribution to maintaining and enhancing the international reputation of Japanese auditing firms (BAC, 2009, pp. 6–7).

Thus, the Interim Report suggested that "Japanese accounting experts should discuss how to deal with IFRS upon sharing their medium- to long-term perspectives" (BAC, 2009, p. 8) and should take action to resolve various issues. The issues to be addressed regarding the application of IFRS were as follows: (1) the quality of IFRS (i.e. the more voice from Japan), (2) the language to be used when applying IFRS (i.e. the translation), (3) due process for setting IFRS (i.e. governance reforms to the IASB/IASCF), and (4) practical measures, including training and education to provide a better understanding of IFRS.

Moreover, the Interim Report indicated the possibility of "carve-outs" in considering the mandatory use of IFRS.

> Furthermore, in making a decision on mandatory application regarding whether to apply IFRS as developed by the IASB or to make partial modifications or exclusions of IFRS, it is necessary to review the content of IFRS and the status of the setting of IFRS (including due process).
>
> (BAC, 2009, p. 18)

In this sense, JMIS can be interpreted as a carve-out, as will be described later. However, Mitsui, who was then in charge of the FSA, provided his personal view that a cautious stance to carve-outs should be taken, saying "a rough-and-ready decision to the carve-out may possibly undercut financial reporting credibility in Japan," and "it requires careful considerations. And thus, rather, we need to strengthen Japan's involvement in the setting of IFRS in a very early stage in order to avoid that situation" (Mitsui, 2009, p. 6).

The acceleration of the possible application of IFRS in the US formed part of the background of this drastic change. The US had been reluctant to implement international accounting standards (Camfferman & Zeff, 2007, 2015), but after the financial reporting crisis from 2001 to 2002 and the Norwalk Agreement, the implementation of IFRS in the US was viewed more positively, and the SEC decided to accept financial statements for foreign private issuers prepared in accordance with IFRS (SEC, 2007). At the same time, the SEC announced that it would determine whether it could allow US issuers to use IFRS by 2011 (SEC, 2008).

Stance of policy makers and constituencies

On August 8, 2007, the day that the Tokyo Agreement was announced, the Keidanren also issued *Advancing the Convergence of Accounting Standards* (Keidanren, 2008a), which displayed a more positive attitude toward the acceptance of IFRS in Japan. The statement reiterated the importance of the EC's equivalence assessment of Japanese GAAP and, especially, the SEC's proposed decision to "accept usage of IFRS without reconciliation to US GAAP in the listing of foreign issuers starting from FY 2009" (Keidanren, 2008a). Thus, the Keidanren speculated as follows:

> If Japan lags behind these international developments, it will not only hinder overseas fundraising by Japanese corporations, but it may also isolate Japanese GAAP from the rest of the world and lead to the lowering of the credibility of Japan's securities market.

The Keidanren therefore argued for further advancement of the convergence of Japanese GAAP with IFRS and US GAAP and proposed four steps to achieve this aim: (1) steadily working to achieve the goals of the EU equivalence assessment of Japanese GAAP based on the ASBJ's Project Plan, (2) setting deadlines for important items beyond those targeted by the equivalence assessment, (3) contributing to the long-term convergence work of the IASB and the FASB, and (4) advancing official mutual recognition between Japan and the EU at the governmental level (Keidanren, 2008a). Moreover, in October 2008, the Keidanren issued a proposal regarding the adoption of IFRS and listed three challenges to overcome in Japan: (1) training and education related to IFRS, (2) full-scale participation in the IFRS development process, and (3) the enhancement of the ASBJ's role (Keidanren, 2008b).

Increasing the voluntary application of IFRS (2011–)

After temporarily taking a cautious stance in 2011 and 2012, the FSA and the BAC regained a positive attitude towards IFRS and sought to create examples of voluntary applications of IFRS. In addition, in examining whether "IFRS were suitable for Japan," the ASBJ issued JMIS, a Japanese version of IFRS.

Domestic and international situation

On March 11, 2011, the Great East Japan Earthquake and the resulting tsunami and nuclear disaster hit northeastern Japan, significantly impacting the Japanese economy. Around this time, accounting experts in Japan temporarily took a cautious stance toward the application of IFRS. However, in December 2012, the LDP won the lower-house election, easily securing a majority, and, thus, Shinzo Abe once again became the head of government (the second Abe Cabinet, 2012–). The atmosphere surrounding the application of IFRS in Japan tremendously changed as a result.

Specifically, the Abe Cabinet announced its intention to increase the number of companies voluntarily adopting IFRS in its growth strategy (COJ, 2014), with a specific goal of 300 companies by the end of 2016. This goal followed a proposal by the Policy Research Council and the Business Accounting Sub-committee of the LDP in June 2013 (LDP, 2013)

Tentative retreat from adoption

After 2009, when the *Interim Report* was issued, the environment surrounding the application of IFRS in Japan drastically changed. Specific changes included: (1) the publication of new SEC Work Plans (February 2010 and May 2011); (2) the extension of the target completion date of the IASB/FASB convergence project beyond June 2011 (April 2011); (3) the publication of a report by the Panel on Non-consolidated Financial Statements of the FASF (April 2011); (4) requests from industrial associations and labor unions (June 2011); (5) an increase in international competition for influence on IFRS, including other competitors from Asia; and (6) the Great East Japan Earthquake. In response to these circumstances, Shozaburo Jimi, the Minister for Financial Service at the time, released *Considerations on the Application of IFRS* (Jimi, 2011) on June 21, 2011. In this statement, he suggested restarting the discussions regarding Japan's adoption of IFRS at the Planning and Coordination Committee in the BAC and postponing the decision regarding the mandatory adoption of IFRS in Japan.[15]

In an interim report of the resumed discussion of the Planning and Coordination Committee, the BAC issued the *Discussion Summary for the Consideration on the Application of IFRS in Japan* (Discussion Summary: BAC, 2012) in July 2012. This document made the following recommendations: (1) more strongly consider the most appropriate way for Japan to respond to IFRS when pursuing convergence between Japanese GAAP and IFRS, (2) build up examples of voluntary applications of IFRS and focus on the purpose of the application of IFRS and its impact on the Japanese economy and legal system, (3) appropriately reflect Japanese opinions in IFRS, and (4) ensure that unlisted small- and medium-sized entities in Japan are not affected by the influence of IFRS (BAC, 2012).

The Present Policy

The BAC issued a report on the use of IFRS in Japan (The Present Policy: BAC, 2013) in June 2013, following the change of government. Like previous BAC statements, the Present Policy reiterated Japan's commitment to establishing a single set of high-quality global accounting standards. However, responding to the LDP proposal (LDP, 2013), it exhibited a more positive attitude and recommended concrete steps or policies for applying IFRS in Japan.

First, the Present Policy proposed relaxing the statutory requirements for eligibility to voluntarily apply IFRS to increase the number of Japanese companies choosing this voluntary application. Specifically, the policy proposed eliminating two requirements: being a listed company in Japan, and conducting financial or business activities internationally. Second, to incorporate IFRS, the Present Policy advocated creating "an endorsement system that examines individual standards from Japan's viewpoint of 'IFRS as they should be' or 'IFRS suitable for Japan'" (BAC, 2013, p. 7).[16] For instance, from the perspective of public interest and investor protection, the Present Policy specifically listed the following three criteria for endorsing individual IFRS standards (BAC, 2013, p. 8):

1   Fundamental philosophy on accounting standards;
2   Difficulties in practice (preparation costs exceed benefits etc.); and
3   Relationship to relevant peripheral regulations (whether various business regulations make it difficult, or cause huge costs to adopt).

Additionally, the Present Policy proposed simplifying the disclosure of non-consolidated (single-entity) financial statements, and it clearly articulated that the policy on the use of different sets of accounting standards for consolidated and non-consolidated financial statements and the policy ensuring that non-listed small and medium-sized entities are unaffected by IFRS "should continue to be maintained" (BAC, 2013, p. 4).

Japan's Modified International Standards (JMIS)

In response to the Present Policy's recommendations, the ASBJ established a Working Group for the Endorsement of IFRS[17] composed of preparers, users, auditors, and researchers. This group held seventeen public meetings. Based on three criteria for "deletion or modification" suggested in the Present Policy, the Working Group discussed thirty issues in particular before eventually focusing on four issues: (1) the non-amortization of goodwill, (2) the recycling of other comprehensive income and profit or loss, (3) the scope of fair value measurement, and (4) the capitalization of development costs.[18]

After these discussions, the ASBJ published the Exposure Draft of JMIS, which focused on the first two issues (ASBJ, 2014). After the comment period, the ASBJ issued *Japan's Modified International Standards (JMIS): Accounting Standards Comprising IFRSs and the ASBJ Modifications* in June 2015. In other words, JMIS refers to a set of accounting standards comprising IFRS, created by the IASB, and two ASBJ modified standard *Accounting for Goodwill* and *Accounting for Other Comprehensive Income*. Thus, similar to other ASBJ standards, JMIS were carved out based on IFRS by a private-sector body, and are legitimized by the FSA, a public-sector body.

JMIS are assumed to have two roles. First, Japan's endorsement of IFRS and JMIS is said to be "a tool" (Tsujiyama, 2014, p. 42) for voicing Japan's fundamental ideas on the application of IFRS or accounting standards in the international arena. Specifically, these ideas include the maintenance of the concept of "profit or loss" with recycling and the periodic amortization of goodwill. The second role of JMIS is to increase the number of Japanese companies that voluntarily adopt IFRS by establishing a transitional (or intermediate) form of IFRS. In other words, the existence of JMIS creates a transition route from Japanese GAAP to JMIS and, then, to IFRS. However, at the time of this writing, although almost 200 Japanese companies have directly adopted pure IFRS, no companies have adopted JMIS, and, thus, JMIS is not the predicted transitional form of IFRS.

Stance of policy makers and constituencies

In May 2011, the representatives of major Japanese companies[19] and the Confederation Union submitted a request to the FSA regarding the application of IFRS. They cited certain countries' (e.g. the US, China, and India) retractions or cautious approaches to the mandatory adoption of IFRS, their anxiety regarding switching costs caused by the mandatory adoption of IFRS, and the fact that the Japanese industry and, moreover, the overall Japanese economy, were not able to bear financial burden after the Great East Japan Earthquake. Thus, they requested an immediate discussion regarding the overall institutional design of the mandatory adoption of IFRS in Japan, including its necessity. Moreover, if this discussion required a substantial amount of time, they requested postponing the final decision regarding the mandatory adoption of IFRS in Japan for an adequate time frame (e.g. five years) or extending the time period in which certain companies were permitted to use US GAAP for their consolidated financial statements.

Responding to the request, the FSA postponed the discussion of the mandatory adoption of IFRS.

After the change in government, however, the Policy Research Council and the Business Accounting Sub-Committee of LDP issued *Statement on Approach to IFRS* in June 2013 (LDP, 2013). Although this statement took a cautious stance regarding the mandatory adoption of IFRS, the LDP stated that, to achieve the "prominent application of IFRS," all available strategies had to be considered to ensure that around 300 companies used IFRS by the end of 2016. Thus, the Abe Cabinet clearly indicated that the "promotion of an increase in the number of companies voluntarily adopting IFRS" (COJ, 2014) was a target for the first time as part of a decision by the cabinet in the Japan Revitalization Strategy in June 2014. Reflecting these circumstances, the Keidanren expressed its support as follows:

> Under the current international situation, it is necessary to maintain the current system in Japanese market where JGAAP, IFRS and U.S. [sic] GAAP coexist. At the same time, measures should be taken to expand the voluntary application of IFRS.
>
> (Keidanren, 2013)

After temporarily taking a cautious stance in 2011 and 2012, the FSA and the BAC regained a positive attitude towards IFRS for "building up the examples of voluntary applications of IFRS" (BAC, 2013, p. 1). However, this attitude toward the application of IFRS in Japan was not intended to promote the mandatory application of IFRS but rather may have resulted from the motivation to maintain or increase Japan's right to voice its opinion (relative political power) in the global arena. For instance, the Present Policy confirmed that Japan's proactive approach to creating a single, high-quality global standard, recommended in the declaration of the G20 Washington Summit, was considered "to be not only useful for Japanese companies to conduct business activities and raise funds, but also important for Japan to ensure the international competitiveness of the Japanese market" (BAC, 2013, p. 2).

In April 2015, the FSA published the *IFRS Adoption Report* (FSA, 2015), which suggested that the number of companies adopting IFRS had been increasing since 2010 and, especially, after 2014, when the cabinet introduced the Japan Revitalization Strategy. Although the report noted that many companies consider "contribution to business management (sophistication of business management)" as the largest merit of IFRS adoption, they faced challenges in the transition to IFRS, such as "treatments of particular accounting standards," especially with regard to accounting issues involving high degrees of estimates and the principles-based nature of IFRS.

Summary

Initially, the ASBJ took a cautious approach to the convergence between Japanese GAAP and IFRS. However, the atmosphere changed following the "Tokyo Agreement" in August 2007, and the situation again shifted remarkably when the FSA and the BAC permitted Japanese companies to voluntarily file consolidated financial statements prepared in agreement with IFRS. After temporarily taking a cautious stance in 2011 and 2012, the FSA and the BAC regained a positive attitude towards IFRS for "building up the examples of voluntary applications of IFRS" (BAC, 2013, p. 1) with the

Table 2.4 Coexistence of four sets of accounting standards in Japan

Standards	Explanation
Japanese GAAP	Japanese generally accepted accounting principles (Japanese GAAP) have been prepared by the national accounting standard-setters, such as the BAC and ASBJ.
US GAAP	US GAAP have been permitted in Japan for companies that are US Securities and Exchange Commission (SEC) registrants or that have been filing consolidated financial statements based on US GAAP to Japanese authorities after 1977.
IFRS (designated IFRS or pure IFRS)	The application of designated IFRS (IFRS endorsed by the minister of the FSA) has been allowed for Japanese companies since December 11, 2009. Designated IFRS are currently adopted for Japanese companies voluntarily. The designation process allows the FSA to not designate certain accounting standards included in pure IFRS, but this process is not designed to modify IFRS as suggested by J-IFRS and JMIS. Thus designated-IFRS is substantially the same as pure IFRS issued by the IASB.
Japan's Modified International Standards (JMIS)	To concretize the original concepts of J-IFRS, suggested by the BAC in 2013, Japan's modified International Standards (JMIS) were suggested by ASBJ, which include the original statements of IFRS, along with the ASBJ's modification standards. The objectives of the development of JMIS include: (1) facilitating more flexible adoption of IFRS for Japanese companies and (2) expressing Japanese constituents' views to the IASB. Specifically, two accounting standards (i.e. accounting standards for goodwill and recycling) were proposed to delete and modify pure IFRS.

Source: Tsunogaya and Tokuga (2015), Table 1, p. 302, modified by authors.

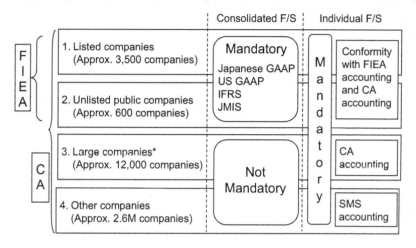

Figure 2.2 Disclosure requirement under the Companies Act (CA) and the Financial Instruments and Exchange Act (FIEA) in Japan

*Companies of which stated capital is 500M JPY or more, or liabilities are 20B JPY or more

Source: Mitsui (2009), Figure 3, modified by authors.

publication of the Present Policy. In addition, the Japanese Cabinet clearly indicated that the "promotion of an increase in the number of companies voluntarily adopting IFRS" was a target for the first time in the Japan Revitalization Strategy (Cabinet Office, 2013, 2014). Table 2.4 and Figure 2.2 show the current situation, in which four sets of accounting standards coexist in Japan.

Notes

1 Cargill and Sakamoto (2008) provide a six-part chronological framework for this period, as follows: (1) the pretransition base incorporating existing economic and political institutions and the implied social contract between the government and citizens (pretransition period); (2) the impact of new economic, political, and technological forces on Japan and Japan's apparent success in adapting its financial system to these new forces (1980 to 1985); (3) the buildup of financial stress, asset price inflation, and the collapse of asset prices (1985 to 1990); (4) economic, financial, and political distress (1990s); (5) a new form of policy making followed by economic and financial recovery (2001 to 2006); and (6) the unraveling of the old social contract between the government and the public and changed to the public's expectations (p. 23).

2 Yamaji, Suzuki, Kajiwara, and Matsumoto (1994) suggest the following relation between economic growth and Japan's accounting system:

> Because of the peculiarity and imperfection of the Japanese capital market, the historical cost principle had been adhered to continuously since the end

of the second World War, and it prevented outflows of appraisal profits to the outside of a company. And thus, this calculation structure of accounting profits had contributed to capital accumulation of businesses in Japan, then an economically undeveloped country.

(p. 33)

3 Here, the term "general investors" refers to future potential investors, whereas the term "current investors" refers to those who are already investing in a listed or unlisted company (Cooke & Kikuya, 1992, p. 174).

4 The BADC, an advisory body of the Ministry of Finance (at that time), deliberated on corporate accounting issues at the request of the Minister. In that sense, the BADC had been the de facto standard-setter in Japan. Initially, the BADC released its accounting standards in the form of Opinions of the Committee with no legal backing. Moreover, although the BADC, a quasi-public-sector standard-setting body, has been the main pillar of this system, it has not actively produced standards, guidance, and interpretations; however, "it spent much time reconciling various accounting requirements of the Codes" (Benston et al., 2006, pp. 167–168).

5 Nederveen Pieterse (2004) describes this new globalization situation as follows:

Contemporary globalization can be described as a package deal that includes informatization (applications of information technology), flexibilization (destandardization in the organization of production and labor), and various changes such as regionalization and the reconfiguration of states. Since the 1980s, the growing impact of neoliberal policies adds to the globalization package, deregulation (liberalization, privatization), marketization (unleashing market forces), financialization and securitization (conversion of assets into tradable financial instruments), and the ideology of lean government.

(Nederveen Pieterse, 2004, p. 1)

6 The Ministry of Finance was reorganized to become the FSA after a series of corruption scandals involving the MOF and the BOJ. This reorganization was "a major institutional change in Japan" (Cargill & Sakamoto, 2008, p. 111). Moreover, the Financial System Reform Law, incorporating most of the reform measures, went into effect on December 1998.

7 See Yonekura, Gallhofer, and Halam (2012) for more details on this initiative.

8 After the bubble economy burst in the early 1990s, a series of bankruptcies of financial institutions occurred, even though "all the different kinds of financial records had been kept by CPA audits, and in all cases there had been clean opinions" (Sakagami et al., 1999, p. 347). In particular, when Yamauchi Securities Co., one of leading securities companies in Japan, voluntarily closed its business, approximately 264 billion yen in off-balance sheet liabilities were revealed ("Shaking Japanese Audit", Nikkey, December 26, 1997). In addition to these hidden losses concealed by Tobashi methods, Trevor (2001) suggests the following problems with traditional Japanese accounting methods: dubious criteria for valuing company assets, the use of auditors inside a firm, and a lack of enforceable independent standards (p. 15).

9 The Second Joint Status Report on the Enhanced Initiative between the US and Japan declared that "enhancement of the disclosure such as shift to the framework of the disclosure primarily based on consolidated accounting" (MOFA, 1999, p. 12).

10 The COFRI was established as a research institution providing assistance to the BADC in July 1990.

11 The Due Process Rules stipulate six steps of due process: agenda setting, technical committee meetings, board meetings, exposure drafts and discussion papers, post-implementation reviews, and reports to the Due Process Oversight Committee.

12 For instance, according to Camfferman and Zeff (2015):

> In terms of overall policy, the view at the FSA and the ASBJ, but also at Nippon Keidanren, the highly influential business federation, was that international convergence of accounting standards should be pursued as a three-way process among IFRSs, Japanese GAAP, and US GAAP, with mutual recognition as a first step.
>
> (Camfferman & Zeff, 2015, p. 82)

13 The FSA finally approved these proposals in December 2009.

14 Specific Companies are those that satisfy the following requirements:

1 Being a listed company in Japan;
2 Having established an appropriate internal framework for IFRS-based consolidated financial reporting; and
3 Conducting financial or business activities internationally.

15 In particular, Jimi (2011) made the following suggestions.

- At the very best, the mandatory application of IFRS should not begin in the fiscal year ending in March 2015, and a sufficient time period (i.e, five to seven years) should be provided for preparation if and after mandatory application is enacted.
- The permission to use US GAAP for disclosure purposes in the interim, that is, through the fiscal year ending on or before March 31, 2016, should not be terminated so that firms can continue their use of US GAAP (Jimi, 2011).

16 Currently, the IFRS used by Japanese companies should be "designated IFRS," which are specified by the commissioner of the FSA. In other words, although the commissioner may choose not to designate some particular pronouncements, "it has been the application of pure IFRS" (Ito, 2013, p. 4) in practice.

17 Japan's endorsement of IFRS, contrary to that of the EU, aims for voluntary application and consists of two alternative approaches. The first approach, led by the FSA, is to approve IFRS as the Designated International Accounting Standards that Japanese companies use for their consolidated financial statements. The second approach, led by the ASBJ, is to delete or modify certain provisions of IFRS.

18 These 30 issues were broadly categorized into two groups: issues for which the fundamental thinking on accounting standards significantly differs, and issues for which promoting the voluntary application of IFRS (including those related to peripheral regulation) is difficult in practice.

19 These companies included Nippon Steel, JFE Holdings, Toyota, Panasonic, Hitachi, Toshiba, etc. (a total of 21 companies), as well as the Japan Chamber of Commerce and Industry (JCCI). Furthermore, in July 2011, the Japanese Trade Union Confederation (*Rengo*) issued action policies in 2012.

3   Interplay between Japan's accounting standards and theories of regulation

Public interest theory

Around the year 2000, Japan faced several external pressures, including the Enhanced Initiative on deregulation and competition policy from the US; the legend clause requirement, which criticized the problems with traditional Japanese accounting and auditing methods; and the EC's equivalence assessment. Thus, restoring confidence in the Japanese accounting system was an urgent task, and its resolution was expected to contribute to the public interest. Specifically, the quality of Japanese GAAP needed to be improved, and differences from international standards (i.e. US GAAP and IFRS) needed to be eliminated.[1] However, domestic industries demanded the continuous use of existing accounting practices, and the resistance to radical changes in accounting standards was intense. Thus, in discussions of accounting regulation reforms in Japan starting in 2000, especially in those regarding the application of IFRS, the private standard-setting body was exposed to various political pressures that were either pro- or anti-IFRS.[2]

Role of the state

In Japan, the FSA, a public regulatory agency, holds the authority for standard setting. The FSA delegates this authority to its advisory body, the BAC, which, in turn, delegates standard setting to the ASBJ, a private-sector entity. In other words, the roles of the BAC and the ASBJ are clearly separated; the former assumes a role in international strategy decisions and an overall stance on standard setting, and the latter plays a role in technical matters. Thus, this arrangement is more of a "functional transfer" (Chiba, 2012, p. 477) than a delegation of authority or an empowerment, as the BAC has little power compared to the US SEC. For that reason, all four sets of accounting standards that Japanese issuers may use for their consolidated financial statements (i.e. Japanese GAAP, IFRS, US GAAP, and JMIS) are formalized into the domestic legal system through *ex post* endorsements by the public sector (e.g. ordinance and public notice), although the standard-setting processes and public delegations sometimes differ (Sanada, 2018). In other words, the delegation of the authority over setting accounting standards to the private sector in Japan is incomplete, and, thus, state intervention remains possible and "the role of state" (Noguchi & Boyns, 2012) is still relevant in standard-setting activities.

As previously mentioned, in 2003, the LDP, which was then the ruling party, made a direct threat against the ASBJ to freeze mark-to-market accounting and suspend the implementation of impairment accounting. In particular, in the case of accounting for fixed asset impairment, the Ministry of Economy, Trade and Industry (METI) was engaged in the deliberation process early (Mori, 2017).

In addition, the Standards Advisory Council (SAC), which was established in May 2007 by the FASF, advises the ASBJ on topics that should be discussed in board meetings regarding both accounting standards and practical solutions. Specifically, the SAC receives and considers proposals for the potential topics from constituencies and, then, decides whether to make a recommendation to the ASBJ. Table 3.1 shows proposed topics received by the SAC. For instance, the SAC received fifteen proposals for the potential accounting standards topics but recommended only two topics for discussion at the ASBJ. These two topics were proposed by the FSA. For practical solutions, the SAC recommended that all five topics proposed by government agencies (i.e. FSA; METI; the Ministry of Agriculture, Forestry and Fisheries; the Ministry of Health, Labour and Welfare; and the Cabinet Office) be discussed at the ASBJ. All of these recommended topics became ASBJ agenda items (see Table 3.1). In this way, government agencies are involved in setting the ASBJ's agenda.

Table 3.1 Numbers of topics discussed and advised by The Standards Advisory Council (as of May 2018)

	Accounting Standards	*Practical Solutions*
Proposals to the SAC	15	31
	Preparers: 4	Preparers: 5
	Users: 4	Users: 3
	Accounting professions: 5	Accounting professions: 18
	Government Agencies: 2	Government Agencies: 5
Advised to the ASBJ	2	19
ASBJ's agenda	2	19

Source: Watabe (2015), modified and updated by authors.

However, the ASBJ deals with this kind of state intervention in a manner that takes a balance of public interests and the interests of a specific industry, while securing its independence.

Balancing: lease accounting

Before the 1990s, Japanese accounting regulations only required lease transactions to be disclosed in a quantitative manner as "real rights" under the provisions of the Commercial Code. In other words, lease transactions were treated similarly to ordinary rental transactions and were considered to be off-balance sheet items. However, when the BADC issued lease accounting standards as part of the *Opinion on Accounting Standards for Lease Transactions* in 1993, it broadly classified lease transactions into two categories: finance lease transactions and operating lease transactions. These standards required finance leases to be recognized as assets and liabilities on the balance sheet (i.e. on-balance sheet treatments) and operating leases to be recognized as expenses on the income statement, rather than as assets or liabilities (i.e. off-balance sheet treatments). This approach was similar to international accounting standards (e.g. IAS 17; SFAS 13) (Kusano, 2019; Kusano & Sakuma, 2019).

However, in Japan, financial leases are further classified into two categories: finance lease transactions that transfer ownership to lessees (FLO) and finance lease transactions that do not transfer ownership to lessees (FLNO). In principle, Japanese firms are required to disclose finance leases on their balance sheets. However, the BADC made an exception allowing Japanese firms to avoid capitalizing FLNO on their balance sheets subject to specific note disclosure requirements to financial statements. Almost all Japanese companies chose this treatment, and, thus, FLNO were not disclosed on firms' balance sheets.[3] In this way, off-balance sheet treatment, or the avoidance of on-balance sheet treatment, remained as an exceptional accounting treatment for FLNO. In other words, in this example, the BADC balanced public interests and the interests of a specific industry, the lease industry in this case.[4]

The ASBJ discussed this exceptional treatment for almost four years before finally issuing ASBJ Statement No. 13 *Accounting Standards for Lease Transactions* and ASBJ Guidance No. 16 Guidance on *Accounting Standards for Lease Transactions* on March 2007. The statement stipulates the following:

> The pre-revision Standard [sic] permitted, subject to specific note disclosure requirements, finance lease transactions that do not transfer ownership to be accounted for in a manner similar to accounting treatment

for ordinary rental transactions. However, such treatment is no longer applicable, and the transactions shall be accounted for in a similar manner with ordinary sale and purchase transactions.

(ASBJ statements No. 13)

Balancing: accounting for business combination

Accounting standards for business combination, together with financial instruments standards, were at the center of the discussion regarding recent revisions to accounting standards. For instance, in the US, the debates about the abolition of the pooling-of-interest method (pooling method) and taking an impairment-only approach to goodwill provide "a window into the political process of accounting rule-making" (Ramanna, 2015, p. 65), which involves Congress, regulators, investment banks, industries, and standard-setting bodies. Similarly, in Japan, the discussion of the convergence of accounting standards for business combinations was, and still is, a "controversial issue that represents the fundamental differences between Japanese GAAP and international accounting standards" (Saito, 2009, p. 303).

In 2003, the BADC issued *Accounting Standards for Business Combination*, the last standards it issued, in view of the circumstances in the US and the IASB. However, the BADC and, later, the ASBJ allowed Japanese firms to continue to use the pooling method under tight restrictions.[5] They did so because of the strong opposition from the business community, which claimed that equal mergers were in the majority of business combinations in Japan. Moreover, the BAC argued that "there was the case when acquirer and acquiree cannot always be identified and it should not be accounted in a uniform manner, contrary to international standards assuming that acquirer and acquiree can always be identified" (Saito, 2004, p. 2). Moreover, according to these standards, goodwill should be amortized systematically on a straight-line basis over the period in which it has an effect for up to a maximum of 20 years, although it should be impaired following the accounting standards for the impairment of fixed assets. In other words, since 2003, goodwill amortization and goodwill impairment have coexisted in Japanese GAAP.

Later, during the global convergence of accounting standards, especially during the EC's equivalence assessment, the ASBJ reconciled these differences, issuing ASBJ Statement No. 21 *Accounting for Business Combination* in December 2008. In this revised standard, the ASBJ abolished the pooling method. However, goodwill amortization and goodwill impairment have continued to coexist. This change was made because the business community may have judged that the planned mergers between large Japanese firms on equal footing were almost completed and would decrease in frequency in the future. In any case, Saito (2009) suggested that "the cost of maintaining the pooling method in Japan has overcome the benefit from the pooling method" (Saito, 2009, p. 306).

Summary

Especially in the 1990s and early 2000s, Japan faced various external pressures to enhance the quality of Japanese GAAP and, thus, to eliminate the difference between Japanese GAAP and US GAAP or IFRS. In addition, as Japanese GAAP and IFRS have converged, Japan has also faced a choice between either the voluntary or mandatory adoption of IFRS. However, domestic industries have demanded the continuous use of existing accounting practices, and intense resistance to radical changes in accounting standards arose. The public interest (or social cost), represented by public authorities, and the private interest (or private cost), represented by private industries, partially conflicted and partially coincided. Thus, the ASBJ, the private-sector standard setter, was exposed to political pressures from various quarters. As a result, balancing public and private interests, the ASBJ chose a compromising approach to standard setting considering the revision processes of US GAAP and IFRS. Moreover, the ASBJ (and the BAC) chose the gradual rather than the rapid reform of accounting standards and left conventional accounting treatments in place.

Capture theory

Our historical narrative suggests that, around 2008, the FSA significantly changed its attitude from a cautious convergence approach to a positive approach that was accepting voluntary IFRS applications and the possible mandatory adoption of IFRS. Drawing on capture theory, we seek to investigate the change exist in its constituencies' actions and conceptions and how these changes affected the BAC and the ASBJ. Specifically, we focus on the Keidanren, a representative pressure group in Japan.

Keidanren

The Keidanren was established in August 1946, immediately following World War II, with the original aim of reconstructing and recovering of the Japanese economy. Now, as a comprehensive economic organization, the Keidanren consists of over 1,000 representative companies and about 150 national and regional industrial associations. Its objective is "to contribute to the self-sustained development of the Japanese economy and the improvement of the lives of citizens, by drawing out the dynamism of corporations as well as that of the individuals and communities that support them" ("About Keidanren", Keidanren website). For this purpose, the Keidanren seeks to establish "consensus in the business community on a variety of important domestic and international issues for their steady and prompt resolution" (*Ibid.*). Regarding corporate disclosures, the Keidanren's Charter of Corporate Behavior suggests, in principle, to "disclose corporate information actively, effectively and fairly and engage in constructive dialogue with a wide range of stakeholders, with a purpose of enhancing corporate value" (Keidanren, 2017).

As stated previously, Japan's attitude shifted significantly from a cautious convergence approach to a more positive stance around 2008. Matsubara and Endo (2018) suggest that the Keidanren drastically evolved from "mutual authentication" to "active acceptance" because the SEC indicated that IFRS adoption in the US was possible. In other words, capture by industrial organizations became possible. The Keidanren may have influenced this shift for several reasons.

First, both the BSC and the ASBJ are deliberative assemblies in which representatives of various stakeholders gather to discuss issues and make decisions. The Keidanren provided an important supply of important, high-quality human resources to these organizations, similar to accounting professionals and academics. Moreover, the Keidanren was a founding member of the ASBJ and played an important role in establishing its legitimacy. Thus, the Keidanren can directly exercise power over the BSC's and ASBJ's decisions through committee members of these organizations.

In addition, the Keidanren has issued policy statements on every aspect of the convergence process (Keidanren, 2003, 2006, 2008b, 2008c, 2013). As mentioned before, these opinions emphasize improving the quality of accounting standards and audits in Japan because of the legend clause issue and essentially seek convergence between Japanese GAAP, US GAAP, and IFRS based on mutual recognition (this stance is in line with those of the BAC and the ASBJ). However, after the Tokyo Agreement in 2007, the Keidanren expressed concerns about Japan's isolation in the global accounting arena owing to the rapid spread of IFRS worldwide, the change in the US's international accounting strategy, and the EC's equivalence assessment. In particular, *Future directions of accounting standards in Japan–The next step towards a single set of accounting standards*, published by the Keidanren in October 2008, marked "a turning-point in the replacement of 'convergence' by 'adoption' in the Japanese dialogue over IFRSs" (Camfferman & Zeff, 2015, p. 519).

This postural change by the Keidanren resulted from changes in the international environment. At the same time, it was caused by changes in the priorities of Japanese companies. For instance, the results of a questionnaire survey conducted by the Keidanren (Keidanren, 2008a) suggest that most Japanese companies have positive opinions regarding the application of IFRS in Japan, although they expressed a diversity of opinions regarding its implementation. Moreover, 67% of the responding companies said that the FSA (and, thus, the BAC) should allow Japanese companies to use IFRS on a voluntary basis. In this way, the Keidanren's opinions impacted and supported the decisions of the BAC and ASBJ.

The Keidanren also engaged in direct and formal lobbying by sending comment letters on exposure drafts issued by the ASBJ. Table 3.2 suggests that 55 out of 1,195 comment letters were sent by the Keidanren, whereas 381 comment letters (31.9%), the largest share, were sent by preparers of financial statements. This phenomenon invites closer analysis, however, we note that industry has great influence over accounting regulation in Japan.

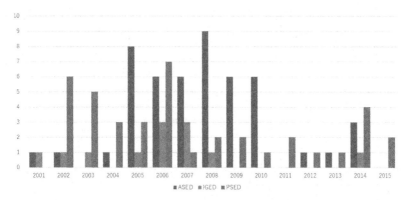

Figure 3.1 Exposure draft (Accounting Standard, Implementation Guidance, and Practical Solutions), 2001–2015

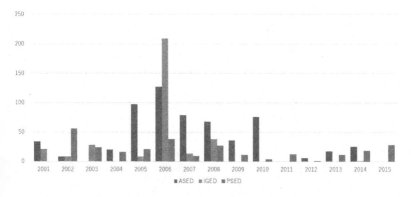

Figure 3.2 Comment letters (Accounting Standard, Implementation Guidance, and Practical Solutions), 2001–2015

Table 3.2 Number of comment letters written by constituent parties to the ASBJ, 2001–2015

	2001	2002	2003	2004	2005	2006	2007	2008	2009	2010	2011	2012	2013	2014	2015	total	ratio
Preparers	15	14	15	12	24	187	30	30	13	15	2	3	7	8	6	381	31.9%
Users	13	15	10	9	31	66	18	42	13	24	0	2	7	12	7	269	22.5%
Accounting profession	24	33	18	13	57	57	36	39	18	32	8	2	9	15	13	374	31.3%
Other profession	1	2	0	0	0	3	0	0	0	0	0	0	0	0	0	6	0.5%
Academics	0	0	1	0	2	7	3	2	1	0	0	0	1	6	1	24	2.0%
Politicians	0	0	0	0	1	0	0	0	0	0	0	0	0	0	0	1	0.1%
Individuals	2	8	8	2	11	54	14	20	2	9	2	0	4	3	1	140	11.7%
total	55	72	52	36	126	374	101	133	47	80	12	7	28	44	28	1195	100.0%

Source: Authors.

Japanese-style management and its ideology

Given the cautious stances and opposition toward the adoption of IFRS in Japan, the Present Policy suggested three concerns: fundamental thinking or philosophy regarding accounting standards, practical difficulties, and the relationship to relevant peripheral regulations (BAC, 2013). In particular, purported differences remain in the fundamental thinking on accounting standards reflected by Japanese GAAP and IFRS. In the forward to JMIS issued in June 2015, the ASBJ specified this difference as follows:

> The fundamental thinking on accounting standards generally accepted in Japan as stated above includes maintaining the usefulness of profit or loss information as an overall indicator of performance. The notion underlying such fundamental thinking is that accounting standards should provide discipline to the entity's management, thereby playing a role in assisting in its sustainable growth and the long-term increase in its corporate value.
>
> (ASBJ, 2015a, par. 10)

Moreover, Camfferman and Zeff (2015) provide a more theoretical explanation for the motive underlying this difference:

> Another challenge to Japanese adoption of IFRSs was the perception, especially in the eyes of manufacturing companies, that in IFRSs the focus was too much on measuring changes in the value of assets and liabilities, at the expense of presenting an entity's performance in terms of the realization concepts. Japanese preparers favoured the revenue-expense approach over the asset-liability approach.
>
> (Camfferman & Zeff, 2015, p. 525)

In the late 1960s, the accounting perspective shifted from economic income measurement (or a measurement approach) to an informational approach (Beaver, 1998, p. 4). Thus, the conceptual framework project conducted by the FASB in the 1970s emphasized that "financial reporting should provide information that is useful to present and potential investors and creditors and other users in making rational investment, credit, and similar decisions" (SFAC No. 1) and supported the asset-liability approach because "the concept of economic income is not well-defined when there are imperfect or incomplete markets for the assets and claims related to the firm" (Beaver, 1998, p. 4). The IASC's conceptual framework was set in 1989 under the influence of the FASB framework. Thus, despite its emphasis on such topics as stewardship, the true and fair view, prudence, and the maintenance of physical capital, its similarities to the FASB framework were "more apparent than the differences" (Camfferman & Zeff, 2007, p. 261). At the same time, the concept of fair value was introduced for the measurement of assets and liabilities in both US GAAP and IFRS.

Under these circumstances, the implementation of IFRS has led to frequent comments that "IFRS are 'fair value based standards' and that the International Accounting Standards Board (IASB) is moving inexorably towards full fair value accounting" and a widespread belief that "IFRS require all assets and liabilities to be measured at fair value and all the resulting changes in fair value to be included as gains and losses in the income statement" (Cairns, 2006, p. 5). This "FV [fair value] myth" (Nobes, 2015, p. 166) and "FVA [fair value accounting] ideology" (Georgiou & Jack, 2011, p. 311), although denied by academic studies (Cairns, 2006; Nobes, 2015) have significantly influenced the debate surrounding the adoption of IFRS in Japan.

The basic assumption of Japanese accounting experts was that accrual accounting (or historical cost accounting), together with Japanese-style management, which included reciprocity or paternalism between management and the workforce, contributed to capital accumulation in the Japanese economy after World War II (Yamaji, Suzuki, Kajiwara, & Matsumoto, 1994). These experts therefore justified "the existing treatment of 'current income' in terms of local business custom, which . . . was appropriately reflected in the Japanese GAAP, but not in IFRS" (Matsubara & Endo, , 2018, pp. 104–105).[6] Thus, in the 2000s, before the voluntary application of IFRS, Japanese accounting experts' beliefs were more in line with the historical cost accounting (HCA) ideology, contrary to the FVA ideology. This ideology or the anti-FVA atmosphere may underpin the LDP's movement to freeze mark-to-market accounting and suspend the implementation of the impairment accounting in 2003.

However, the convergence between Japanese GAAP and IFRS (and US GAAP) has inevitably infiltrated fair value measurements and disclosures into Japanese GAAP and, thus, into accounting treatments in Japan. With the extended use of fair value measurements in accounting practices, preparers and users of financial statements in Japan have grown accustomed to them and have begun to take them for granted. As a result, their beliefs and attitudes were encouraged to change, and anti-FVA movements, like those that occurred in the early 2000s, have largely ceased. In other words, the progress of the mixed attribute accounting model has led not to purification of the FVA and HCA ideology, but to the hybridization of two ideologies. As a result, "fluctuations" in the HCA ideology have occurred.

Cultural theory

Traditionalists and internationalists have conflicted in the Japanese political arena, and decisions are based on a consensus reached through *nemawashi*, an informal process for arriving at a consensus by persuading the people involved. Thus, reaching a final consensus regarding IFRS implementation took significant time. Moreover, Japanese culture is characterized by ambiguity, and, thus, the coexistence of four sets of accounting standards in Japan remains a tentative solution and reflects this ambiguity.

Conflict between traditionalists and internationalists

The modern development of Japan after the Meiji Restoration is described as a process of imitation and emulation with original innovation: "Meiji Japan is so remarkable for the apparent voluntarism of its emulation of foreign organizational forms and for the speed and scope of its borrowing that it is sometimes considered to be unique" (Westney, 1987, p. 12). Similarly, the post-war reform of Japanese institutions followed the US model, but, over time, these institutions' operations returned to the patterns embedded in Japanese culture (Harrison & McKinnon, 1986). For instance, the development of business accounting in Japan after World War II can be viewed as a process through which Business Accounting Principles, issued through a special political process under the occupation of the General Headquarters of the Allied Forces, were adapted and assimilated the current economic situation in Japan (Yamaji et al., 1994, p. 17). It was also a reflexive process in which "Japan formed a new domestic institution based on its traditions by greedily absorbing foreign practices, and it formed another institution by blending domestic and foreign practices" (Tsumori, 2002, pp. 323–324). In this process, internationalists, or the international school (proponents), and traditionalists (opponents) have always been in conflict.

In the context of accounting standards, the internationalists are quite simple because they always take a pro-American or pro-IASB stance, although their opinions differed regarding convergence toward or the full adoption of IFRS. On the contrary, the traditionalists are somewhat more complex because they range from dogmatic traditionalists, who cling to existing accounting practices (i.e. the HCA ideologists), to hidden reformists, who use "the increasing institutional pressures from abroad ("*gaiatsu*") as an impetus rather passively responding to them" (Tsumori,2002, p. 345) in the emulation process. Moreover, the extended use of fair value accounting in Japanese GAAP has, if anything, encouraged changes in traditionalists' beliefs and ideologies.

In the conflict regarding the implementation of mark-to-market and impairment accounting, which were both quite different from Japan's traditional accounting practices, the LDP's Committee of Financial Affairs and the METI, which represented a portion of the industry, exerted pressure on the ASBJ, although the cabinet and the FSA supported the ASBJ. As users of financial statements, the banking and life insurance industries opposed these accounting measures, but accounting professionals (e.g. JICPA) expressed support. Moreover, the Japan Chamber of Commerce and Industry (JCCI), most of whose members are small- and medium-sized enterprises, opposed these measures, whereas the Keidanren, most of whose members are large firms, supported them. Therefore, this conflict was not merely a confrontation between a conservative party and a private-sector standard-setting body, but rather represented a multi-layered and complicated confrontation between the globalization of accounting standards and nationalism in the political economy that took place among the setter of accounting standards and its constituencies, political parties, and the government.

As there has always been conflict between traditionalists and internationalists in the Japanese political arena, decisions are based on a consensus reached through *nemawashi* (an informal process for arriving at a consensus by persuading the people involved). Thus, reaching a final consensus regarding controversial issues, such as the application of IFRS, takes a significant amount of time. In some cases, reaching this consensus required outreach to potential opponents, such as public relations through the ASBJ website, publications, and other workshops.

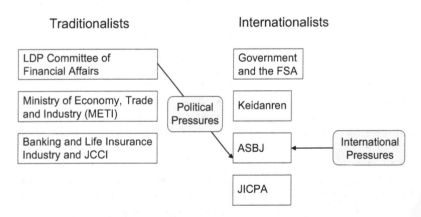

Figure 3.3 Conflict in the discussion of the postponement of the mark-to-market and impairment accounting

Source: Authors refer to Ishikawa (2006) and Mori (2017).

The ASBJ's online public relations include internet broadcasts of its board meetings, periodic uploads of the "ASBJ Newsletter," and the provision of the "ASBJ Web Seminar" for users and preparers of financial statements. The ASBJ also publishes *Accounting Standards & Disclosure Quarterly* four times a year (a total of 51 volumes as of the end of 2015), instruction papers, and other related papers in a timely manner. Furthermore, it has held various seminars expounding at length on newly issued standards (e.g. FASF seminars, basic courses in disclosure, accounting standards exposi- tions, points of debate, and hearings), debriefs on ASBJ and FASF activities (e.g. lectures, open conferences, and debriefing sessions), and commentar- ies on international trends in accounting standard setting (e.g. international conferences, open seminars, panel discussions, and symposia). Table 3.3 provides details regarding the frequency of these workshops and suggests that most outreach activities were concentrated 2003. Only FASF semi- nars and open seminars have been held in later years. The growing use of the internet (e.g. web seminars) and the further specialization of technical issues due to the completion of basic standards have reduced the need for workshops for general users and preparers.

Ambiguity

Japanese culture is characterized by ambiguity (Oe, 1995), and ambiguous settlements and postponements of decisions are common. Thus, the com- plex and confusing decision to allow four sets of accounting standards to coexist in Japan reflects this ambiguity, and it is merely a tentative solution. However, this decision was context-sensitive, and, in that sense, we can identify some rationality behind this complexity.

The FSA continued to allow Japanese companies to use US GAAP for their consolidated financial statements, even though it once suggested abol- ishing this treatment in 2015 or 2016. This change was primarily because of political pressure from Japanese industries during the financial turmoil after the Great East Japan Earthquake. However, since the 2000s, the number of Japanese companies listed on the New York Stock Exchange (NYSE) has continued to decrease from more than twenty to eleven companies in 2018 (at the time of this writing). Moreover, nine of the eleven companies delisted from the NYSE since 2006 have switched to IFRS (see Tables 3.4 and 3.5).

Environmental changes and changes in international accounting policies have occurred in the US, underpinning this decline. First, as the globaliza- tion of financial markets has intensified, Japanese companies have increas- ingly raised funds overseas through other financial arrangements besides share issuances. Thus, Japanese companies' needs to bear the costs of over- seas listings have decreased. Moreover, as the convergence between US

Table 3.3 ASBJ Workshops

	2001	2002	2003	2004	2005	2006	2007	2008	2009	2010	2011	2012	2013	2014	2015	total
FASF Seminar	1	2	2	1	2	3	2	3	3	2	2	2	3	2	2	32
Basic course in disclosure		4	12	1												17
Accounting standards exposition		2	2	1		1										6
Point of debate			2													2
Hearing			1													1
Lecture		3	1	1		1										6
Open conference		1	1	1	1	1										5
Debriefing session			1	1												2
International conference						1										1
Open seminar				1			1	2	1	3	3	3	2	1	1	18
Panel discussion	1															1
Symposium		1	1	1												3
total	2	13	23	8	3	7	3	5	4	5	5	5	5	3	3	94

Source: corrected by authors from ASBJ/FASF 10 years history (2000–2011) and Accounting Standards & Disclosure Quarterly (2012–2015).

Table 3.4 Japanese listed companies on the NYSE (as of November 2018)

Company Name	Ticker	Listed Date	Adopting Standards
Sony Corporation	SNE	9/17/1970	US GAAP
Honda Motor Co., Ltd.	HMC	2/11/1977	IFRS*
MUFG Bank, Ltd.	MUFG	9/19/1989	US GAAP
ORIX Corporation	IX	9/18/1998	US GAAP
Toyota Motor Corporation	TM	9/29/1999	US GAAP
Canon Inc.	CAJ	9/14/2000	US GAAP
Nomura Holdings Inc.	NMR	12/17/2001	US GAAP
Mizuho Financial Group, Inc.	MFG	11/8/2006	US GAAP
Sumitomo Mitsui Financial Group, Inc.	SMFG	11/1/2010	US GAAP
LINE Corporation	LN	7/14/2016	IFRS**

*Switched from FY 2014

**Switched from FY 2015

Source: Authors.

Table 3.5 Delisted Japanese companies from the NYSE (as of November 2018)

Company Name	Ticker	Listed Date	Delisted Date	Switching to IFRS from
Pioneer Corporation	PIO	1976	1/2006	–
TDK Corporation	TDK	1982	4/2009	–
Hitachi, Ltd.	HIT	4/14/198	4/27/2012	FY 2014
Panasonic Corporation	PC	9/1971	4/2013	FY 2016
KUBOTA Corporation	KUB	11/9/1976	7/16/2013	FY2018
KONAMI Holding Corporation	KNM	9/30/2002	4/24/2015	FY 2014
ADVANTEST Corporation	ATE	9/17/2001	4/22/2016	FY 2015
Nidec Corporation	NJ	9/27/2001	5/2/2016	FY 2016
Nippon Telegraph and Telephone Corporation	NTT	9/29/199	4/3/2017	FY2018
NTT DOCOMO, Inc.	DCM	3/1/2002	4/13/2018	FY2018
KYOCERA Corporation	KYO	5/23/1980	6/26/2018	FY2018

Source: Authors refer to Japan Exchange Group, web page. Available at www.jpx.co.jp/listing/others/ifrs/index.html

GAAP and IFRS has progressed and the SEC permits foreign issuers in the US market to use IFRS, the cost of switching from US GAAP to IFRS that Japanese companies must bear has decreased. In other words, because this switching cost is a function of time and environmental changes, an ambiguous or extended decision has created late-comer advantages, and, thus, is somewhat rational.[7]

Seen from this perspective, JMIS provides an interesting example, especially for international scholars. As of December 2018, no firms are using JMIS for their consolidated financial statements, and, thus, JMIS does not function as accounting standards. Although JMIS is said to be "a tool" (Tsujiyama, 2014, p. 42) to voice Japan's fundamental ideas regarding the application of IFRS and accounting standards in the international arena, it may also be a "tool" to avoid criticism from the IASB that JMIS refers to carve-outs from pure IFRS by retaining JMIS as domestic accounting standards set by the ASBJ, a private-sector body. In addition, JMIS may be interpreted as a reconciliatory measure for domestic traditionalists who insist on the maintenance of goodwill amortization and the recycling of other comprehensive income.

Summary

In Japan, the delegation of the authority for setting accounting standards to the private sector is incomplete, and, thus, the role of the public sector is still important. Throughout the 2000s, Japan had continued to enhance the quality of Japanese GAAP in response to repeated external pressures to achieve the global convergence of accounting standards and to secure Japan's status within the international accounting arena for the public interest. However, the public sector also had to acknowledge the costs of the continuous changes in accounting standards to Japanese companies. Although public and private interests partially conflicted and partially coincided, the ASBJ was exposed to political pressures from various quarters. Thus, Japan's reformation of accounting regulations during this era was revolutionary at times and evolutionary at other times in striking a balance between public and private interests.

The Keidanren was (and still is) one of the most influential groups over the decisions by the BAC and ASBJ in Japan. Initially, the Keidanren took a cautious stance regarding the adoption of IFRS. However, owing to the progress made toward convergence between Japanese GAAP and IFRS (and US GAAP) and the resulting co-evolution of related institutions, the switching cost to IFRS borne by Japanese companies declined, and their beliefs (i.e. the HCA ideology) have changed. Thus, the Keidanren changed its attitude and became an active advocate of the adoption of IFRS. The further acceleration of the voluntary adoption of IFRS therefore took place under the initiative of the Keidanren.

The coexistence of four sets of accounting standards in Japan appears at first glance to be an ambiguous settlement or a postponement of a decision. However, the conflict between internationalists and traditionalists underpins this decision. Moreover, as the switching cost is a function of time and environmental changes, this ambiguous or extended decision has created late-comer advantages, and, thus, this co-existence, as a complicated institutional apparatus that reconciles various contradictory interests, has some rationality behind its ambiguity.

Notes

1 These two benchmarks, however, were moving targets that continued to change because the convergence projects of the FASB and the IASB were still ongoing.
2 Although public interest theory justifies state interventions, these circumstances call into question the independence of the ASBJ.
3 Referring to a report by the Japan Leasing Association (JLA, 2003), Kusano and Sakuma (2019) suggest that "99.7 % of Japanese listed companies that prepared consolidated financial statements following Japanese GAAP chose the off-balance sheet treatment of FLNO" (Kusano & Sakuma, 2019, p. 55, footnote 2).
4 Tsumori (2002) refers to such situations as the coexistence of "regulation" and "regulation avoidance."
5 These permissions were only granted for "operations in which the acquirer could not be identified" (Garcia, 2011, p. 60).
6 Tsumori (1995) suggests that the business philosophy of all Japanese companies since the Meiji Restoration in 1868 was the "principle of the traditional paternalistic domination of business," and thus, based on this principle, accounting had been considered a "private instrument for the dominators of business" or a "system to protect business secrets" (Tsumori, 1995: 74).
7 For instance, the Interim Report (BAC, 2009) lists the following issues that must be resolved for the application of IFRS in Japan: the quality of IFRS, the language to be used for the application of IFRS, due process for setting IFRS, and practical measures, such as training and education to ensure a better understanding of IFRS. However, most of these issues have been resolved while gaining sufficient experience with the voluntary application of IFRS.

Conclusions

Summary of our findings

In this study, we aimed to provide international readers insights into the unique coexistence of four sets of consolidated accounting standards in Japan. We first developed two research questions regarding the causal process leading to this coexistence and its theoretical implications. To answer these questions, we sought to construct a historical narrative of the interplay between Japan's accounting standards and theories of regulation. Specifically, we first investigated the reasons that four sets of accounting standards coexist in Japan and their necessity or inevitability using an explaining-outcome process-tracing method. Then, we presented a minimally sufficient explanatory hypothesis for the coexistence of four sets of accounting standards in Japan drawing on the framework of regulation theory.

Our historical narrative shows that the BAC and the ASBJ initially sought mutual recognition and took a cautious approach to the convergence of Japanese GAAP and IFRS. However, the Tokyo Agreement in August 2007 changed the atmosphere surrounding accounting standards, and the situation changed to a remarkable degree when the FSA and BAC permitted Japanese companies to voluntarily file consolidated financial statements prepared in agreement with IFRS. Some background factors, such as the EC's equivalence assessments and changes in attitude toward IFRS in the US, also caused changes in Japanese constituencies' attitudes. Thus, after taking a temporarily cautious stance in 2011 and 2012, the FSA and the BAC regained positive attitudes toward IFRS and sought to create examples of voluntary applications of IFRS with great urgency. At the same time, JMIS were introduced as "a tool" (Tsujiyama, 2014, p. 42) to voice Japan's fundamental ideas regarding the application of IFRS and accounting standards in the international arena.

Our theoretical analysis suggests that public interests (i.e. the restoration of confidence in the Japanese accounting system through convergence with international accounting standards) and private interests (i.e. switching costs owed by Japanese companies) partially conflicted and partially coincided, and, thus, the ASBJ was exposed to political pressures from various quarters. The reformation of accounting regulations in Japan in the 2000s was therefore both revolutionary and evolutionary in balancing public and private interests. Furthermore, the Keidanren, one of the most influential pressure groups in Japan, initially took a cautious stance toward the adoption of IFRS. However, as the convergence process progressed, leading to the co-evolution of related institutions, the cost of switching to IFRS borne by Japanese companies declined. Thus, the Keidanren changed its stance and actively advocated for the adoption of IFRS. The coexistence of four sets of accounting standards in Japan appears to be an ambiguous settlement and a postponement of a decision. However, a conflict between internationalists and traditionalists underpinned this ambiguity. Moreover, as the switching cost was a function of time and environmental changes, the ambiguous or extended decision brought late-comer advantages. Thus, through this analysis, we have succeeded in identifying some rationality behind the co-existence of four accounting standards in Japan.

Value and contributions

This study contributes to the body of knowledge on this topic in several ways. First, it contributes to the historical literature. We provide a historical overview of the recent developments in accounting regulations in Japan, with which international readers are not necessarily familiar. Moreover, much historical analysis uses inductive or descriptive approaches for Japanese cases. Drawing on theories of regulation, we suggest a possible deductive, or theoretically informed, historical analysis. Second, this study contributes to the comparative literature. Although case studies of countries that do not apply IFRS are still few or premature, this study provides a valuable detailed case study of a country that does not apply IFRS. Finally, this study provides a timely response to the policy debates in Japan, which have been rapidly changing.

Future challenges

This study's findings suggest several directions for future research. First, this study provides a detailed description of Japan's unique accounting regulation experience. However, the potential results of this coexistence of accounting standards (e.g. the continuation of this situation or the full adoption of IFRS) are still unclear. Thus, it will be necessary to closely monitor the status of the application of IFRS in Japan. Second, the impact of changes to the international environment on accounting regulations in Japan will be an important research area because the restructuring of accounting regulations in Japan, especially after the accounting big bang, is "a complicated issue which we must examine in the indigenous context of Japan, at the same time, which is requiring us to pay careful attention to the international trends that define this process at the bottom" (Tsumori, 2002, p. 354). Third, future research is needed to conduct a comparative study including other regions and jurisdictions.

More specifically, from the perspective of public interest theory, more detailed examinations of the role of the state, government agency interventions, and the significance of administration changes will provide fertile grounds for future study. Despite the existence of industrial capture in accounting standard setting, this study lacks a detailed consideration of direct lobbying through submissions of comment letters, and, thus, future research should utilize more sophisticated qualitative methods (e.g. content analysis, narrative analysis, etc.) to examine constituents' participation in the standard-setting process in Japan. Furthermore, future research should perform a more detailed analysis of the origin of the historical-cost ideology in Japan and a theoretical consideration of its conflicts with the FVA ideology.

Finally, a comprehensive history of accounting regulations in Japan that includes developments before 2000 would be a major contribution to historical research in accounting, as synthetic compounds consist of various variables, such as the unique development of political economics (i.e. post-war reconstruction, high economic growth, the collapse of the bubble economy and the subsequent recession, and the economic recovery), influence from abroad (particularly from the US), and culture.

Bibliography

Ahmed, K., Chalmers, K., & Khlif, H. (2013). A meta-analysis of IFRS adoption effects. *The International Journal of Accounting, 48,* 173–217.

Albu, C. N., Albu, N., & Alexander, D. (2014). When global accounting standards meet local context: Insights from an emerging economy. *Critical Perspectives on Accounting, 25*(6), 489–510.

Aleinikoff, T. A. (1987). Constitutional law in the age of balancing. *The Yale Law Journal, 96*(5), 943–1005.

Allison, G., & Zelikow, P. (1999). *Essence of decision: Explaining the Cuban missile crisis.* 2nd ed. New York: Longman. (originally published in 1971)

American Accounting Association's Financial Accounting Standards Committee (AAA FASC). (1999). Response to IASC discussion paper: Shaping IASC for the Future. *Accounting Horizons, 13*(4), 223–452.

Aoki, M. (2010). *Corporations in evolving diversity: Cognition, governance, and institutions.* Oxford, UK: Oxford University Press.

Armstrong, C. S., Barth, M. E., Jagolinzer, A. D., & Riedl, E. J. (2010). Market reaction to the adoption of IFRS in Europe. *The Accounting Review, 85*(1), 31–61.

Baker, C. R., & Barbu, E. M. (2007). Trends in research on international accounting harmonization. *The International Journal of Accounting, 27,* 272-304.

Barth, M. E. (2006). Research, standard setting, and global financial reporting. *Foundation and Trends in Accounting, 1*(2), 71–165.

Barth, M. E., Landsman, W. R., & Lang, M. H. (2008). International accounting standards and accounting quality. *Journal of Accounting Research, 46*(3), 467–498.

Baudot, L. (2014). Perspectives on the role of and need for accounting regulation. In C. Mourik & P. Walton (Eds.), *The Routledge companion to accounting, reporting and regulation* (pp. 207–245). New York: Routledge.

Baudot, L., & Walton, P. (2014). Influence on the standard-setting and regulatory process. In C. Mourik & P. Walton (Eds.), *The Routledge companion to accounting, reporting and regulation* (pp. 318–338). New York: Routledge

Beach, D., & Pedersen, R. B. (2013). *Process-tracing methods: Foundations and guidelines.* Ann Arbor, MI: The University of Michigan Press.

Beaver, W. H. (1998). *Financial reporting: An accounting revolution.* 3rd ed. Upper Saddle River, NJ: Prentice-Hall.

Bengtsson, E. (2011). Repoliticalization of accounting standard setting: The IASB, the EU and the global financial crisis. *Critical Perspectives on Accounting, 22,* 567–580.

Bennett, A., & Checkel, J. T. (2015). Process tracing: From philosophical roots to best practices. In A. Bennett & J. T. Checkel (Eds.), *Process tracing: From metaphor to analytic tool* (pp. 3–38). Cambridge, UK: Cambridge University Press.

Benston, G. J., Bromwich, M., Litan, R. E., & Wagenhofer, A. (2006). *World wide financial reporting: The development and future of accounting standards*. Oxford, UK: Oxford University Press.

Bernstein, M. (1955). *Regulating business by independent commission*. Princeton, NJ: Princeton University Press.

Bischof, J., & Daske, H. (2016). Interpreting the European Union's IFRS endorsement criteria: The case of IFRS 9. *Accounting in Europe, 13*(2), 129–168.

Botzem, S. (2012). *The politics of accounting regulation: Organizing transnational standard setting in financial reporting*. Cheltenham, UK: Edward Elgar.

Botzem, S. (2015). *The European Union's role in international economic fora, paper 7: The IASB*. Directorate General for Internal Policies, Policy Department A: Economic and Scientific Policy, IP/A/ECON/2014-15 PE 592.196, European Parliament, June 2015.

Bratton, W. W. (2006). *Private standards, public governance: A new look at the Financial Accounting Standards Board*. Retrieved from SSRN http://ssrn.com/abstract=902905.

Breyer, S. (1982). *Regulation and its reform*. Cambridge, MA: Harvard University Press.

Brüggemann, U., Hitz, J. M., & Sellhorn, T. (2013). Intended and unintended consequences of mandatory IFRS adoption: A review of extant evidence and suggestions for future research. *European Accounting Review, 22*(1), 1–37.

Bryman, A. (2016). *Social research methods*. 5th ed. Oxford, UK: Oxford University Press.

Büthe, T. (2010). *The dynamics of principals and agents: Institutional persistence and change in U.S. financial regulation, 1934–2003*, March 1, 2010. Retrieved from SSRN https://ssrn.com/abstract=1796542

Büthe, T., & Mattli, W. (2011). *The new global rulers: The privatization of regulation in the world economy*. Princeton, NJ: Princeton University Press.

Cairns, D. (2006). The use and evolution of fair value in IFRS. *Accounting in Europe, 3*(1), 5–22.

Camfferman, K., & Detzen, D. (2018). "Forging accounting principles" in France, Germany, Japan, and China: A comparative review. *Accounting History, 23*(4), 448–486.

Camfferman, K., & Zeff, S. A. (2007). *Financial reporting and global capital markets: A history of the International Accounting Standards Committee, 1973–2000*. Oxford: Oxford University Press.

Camfferman, K., & Zeff, S. A. (2015). *Aiming for global accounting standards: The International Accounting Standards Board, 2001–2011*. Oxford: Oxford University Press.

Cargill, T. F., & Sakamoto, T. (2008). *Japan since 1980*. Cambridge, UK: Cambridge University Press.

Christensen, H. B., Hail, L., & Leuz, C. (2013). Mandatory IFRS reporting and changes in enforcement. *Journal of Accounting and Economics, 56*(1–2), 147–177.

Coase, R. (1937). The nature of firm. *Economica, 4*(16), 386–405.

Cooke, T. E., & Kikuya, M. (1992). *Financial reporting in Japan: Regulation, practice and environment.* Oxford, UK: Blackwell.

Cooper, D. J., & Robson, K. (2006). Accounting, professions and regulation: Locating the sites of professionalization, *Accounting, Organizations and Society, 31,* 415–444.

Daske, H., Hail, L., Leuz, C., & Verdi, R. (2008). Mandatory IFRS reporting around the world: Early evidence on the economic consequences. *Journal of Accounting Research, 46*(5), 1085–1142.

Daske, H., Hail, L., Leuz, C., & Verdi, R. (2013). Adopting a label: Heterogeneity in the economic consequences around IAS/IFRS adoptions. *Journal of Accounting Research, 51*(3), 495–547.

De George, E. T., Li, X., & Shivakumar, L. (2016). A review of the IFRS adoption literature. *Review of Accounting Studies, 21,* 898–1004.

Dewing, I., & Russell, P. O. (2008). Financial integration in EU: The first phase of EU endorsement of international accounting standards. *Journal of Common Market Studies, 46*(2), 243–264.

Dore, R. (1987). *Taking Japan seriously: A Confucian perspective on leading economic issues.* London: Athlone Press

Doron, M. E. (2016). The Securities Acts and public accounting: Financial statement audit as symbolic reform. *Accounting History, 21*(2–3), 329–343.

Doupnik, T. S., & Salter, S. B. (1995). External environment, culture and accounting practice: A preliminary test of a general model of international accounting development. *International Journal of Accounting, 30*(2), 189–207.

Durocher, S., Fortin, A., & Côté, L. (2007). Users' participation in the accounting standard-setting process: A theory-building study. *Accounting Organizations and Society, 32,* 29–59.

European Parliament and the Council of the European Union (EU). (2002). The IAS Regulation (EC) No. 1606/2002 of the European Parliament and the Council of 19 July 2002 on the Application of International Accounting Standards. *Official Journal of the European Union.*

FASB. (1999). *International Accouting Standard Setting: A vision for the future. report of the FASB.* Norwalk: FASB.

FASB. (2011). *Progress report on IASB-FASB convergence work, 21 April 2011.* Norwalk: FASB.

Fédération des Experts Comptables Européens (FEE). (2001, April). *Enforcement mechanisms in Europe: A preliminary investigation of oversight systems.*

Financial Accounting Foundation (FAF). (2008). *Financial Accounting Foundation, 2008 annual report.* Norwalk: FAF.

Financial Times. (1997). (Alice in) 'Wonderland accounting'. Leading article. *Financial Times,* London, November 26, 1997.

Fleckner, A. M. (2008). FASB and IASB: Dependence despite independence. *Virginia Law & Business Review, 3*(2), 275–309.

Garcia, C. (2011). A brief history of accounting for goodwill in Japan and France: War, tax and accounting practice. *Keizai-Ronshu (The Economic Review of Gakushuin University), 48*(1), 45–64.

George, A. L., & Bennett, A. (2005). *Case studies and theory development in the social sciences*. Cambridge, MA: MIT Press.

Georgiou, O., & Jack, L. (2011). In pursuit of legitimacy: A history behind fair value accounting. *The British Accounting Review, 43*, 311–323.

Gernon, H., & Meek, G. K. (2001). *Accounting: An international perspective*. 5th ed. New York: Irwin/McGraw-Hill.

Giner, B. (2018). *The politics of accounting: A European perspective*. Speech at the Sixth International Conference of the Journal of International Accounting Research (JIAR), Venice, Italy, June 29, 2018.

Giner, B., & Arce, M. (2012). Lobbying on accounting standards: Evidence from IFRS 2 on share-based payments. *European Accounting Review, 21*(4), 655–691.

Gray, S. J. (1988). Toward a theory of cultural influence on the development of accounting systems internationally. *ABACUS, 24*(1), 1–15.

Guerreiro, M. S., Rodrigues, L. L., & Craig, R. (2012). Voluntary adoption of International Financial Reporting Standards by large listed companies in Portugal: Institutional logics and strategic responses. *Accounting, Organizations and Society, 37*(7), 482–499.

Hail, L., & Leuz, C. (2007). International differences in the cost of equity capital: Do legal institutions and securities regulation matter? *Journal of Accounting Research, 44*(3), 485–531.

Hail, L., Leuz, C., & Wysocki, P. (2010), Global accounting convergence and the potential adoption of IFRS by the U.S. (Part 1): Conceptual underpinnings and economic analysis, *Accounting Horizons, 24*(3), 355–394.

Harrison, G. L., & McKinnon, J. L. (1986). Culture and accounting change: A new perspective on corporate reporting regulation and accounting policy formulation. *Accounting, Organization and Society, 11*(3), 233–252.

Hiramatsu, K. (1988). Group accounting in Japan. In S. H. Gray, A. Coenenberg, & P. Gordon (Eds.), *International group accounting*. London: Routledge.

Holthausen, R. W. (2009). Accounting standards, financial reporting outcomes, and enforcement. *Journal of Accounting Research, 47*(2), 447–458.

Hopwood, A. G. (1987). The archaeology of accounting systems. *Accounting, Organizations and Society, 12*(3), 207–234.

IFRS Foundation (IFRSF). (2016). *IFRS application around the world – Jurisdiction profile: Japan* (last updated on July 28, 2016). Retrieved March 13, 2017 from www.ifrs.org/Use-around-the-world/Documents/Jurisdiction-profiles/Japan-IFRS-Profile.pdf

IFRS Foundation (IFRSF). (2017). *Analysis of the IFRS jurisdiction profiles* (last updated on February 24, 2017). Retrieved March 13, 2017 www.ifrs.org/use-around-the-world/pages/jurisdiction-profiles.aspx

Institute of Chartered Accountants in England and Wales (ICAEW). (2014, October). *The effects of mandatory IFRS adoption in the EU: A review of empirical research*. Financial Reporting Faculty of the Institute of Chartered Accountants in England and Wales.

Johnson, S. B., & Solomons, D. (1984). Institutional legitimacy and the FASB. *Journal of Accounting and Public Policy, 3*,165–183.

Jorissen, A., Lybaert, N., Orens, R., & Van Der Tas, L. (2012). Formal participation in the IASB's due process of standard setting: A multi-issue/multi-period analysis. *European Accounting Review, 21*(4), 693–729.

Kikuya, M. (2001). International harmonization of Japanese accounting standards. *Accounting, Business & Financial History, 11*(3), 349–368.

Kimura, So, & Ogawa, H. (2007). A model for the convergence of accounting standards. *Research in Accounting Regulation, 19*, 215–229.

Koga, C., & Rimmel, G. (2007). Accounting harmonisation and diffusion of international accounting standards: The Japanese case. In J. M. Godfrey & K. Chalmers (Eds.), *Globalisation of accounting standards* (pp. 218–237). Cheltenham, UK: Edward Elgar.

Kothari, S. P., Ramanna, K., & Skinner, D. J. (2010). Implication for GAAP from an analysis of positive research in accounting. *Journal of Accounting and Economics, 50*, 246–286.

Kusano, M. (2019). Recognition versus disclosure of finance leases: Evidence from Japan. *Journal of Business Finance & Accounting, 2019*, 1–24. Retrieved from https://doi.org/10.1111/jbfa.12366

Kusano, M., & Sakuma, Y. (2019). Effects of recognition versus disclosure of finance leases on audit fees and costs: Evidence from Japan. *Journal of Contemporary Accounting & Economics, 15*, 53–68.

Kvaal, E. & Nobes, C. (2010). International differences in IFRS policy choice: A research note. *Accounting and Business Research, 40*(2), 173–187.

Langley, A. (1999). Strategies for theorizing from process data. *Academy of Management Review, 24*(4), 671–710.

Leuz, C. (2010). Different approaches to corporate reporting regulation: How jurisdictions differ and why. *Accounting and Business Research, 40*(3), 229–256.

Leuz, C., & Wysocki, P. (2016). The economic consequences of financial reporting and disclosure regulation: A review and suggestions for future research. *Journal of Accounting Research, 54*(2), 525–621.

Li, S. (2010). Does mandatory adoption of international accounting standards reduce the cost of equity capital? *The Accounting Review, 85*(2), 607–636.

Linsley, P., McMurray, R., & Shirives, P. (2016). Consultation in the policy process: Douglasian cultural theory and the development of accounting regulation in the face of crisis. *Public Administration, 94*(4), 988–1004.

Linsley, P., & Shirives, P. (2014). Douglasian cultural dialogues and the financial reporting council complexity project. *Critical Perspectives on Accounting, 25*, 757–770.

Maruyama, M. (1963). *Thought and behaviour in modern Japanese politics*. Oxford, UK: Oxford University Press.

Matsubara, S., & Endo, T. (2018). The role of local accounting standard setters in institutional complexity: "Explosion" of local standards in Japan. *Accounting, Auditing & Accountability Journal, 31*(1), 96–111.

Mattli, W., & Büthe, T. (2005). Global private governance: Lessons from a national model of setting standards in accounting. *Law and Contemporary Problems, 68*, 225–62.

Merino, B. D., & Mayper, A. G. (2001). Securities legislation and the accounting profession in the 1930s: The rhetoric and reality of the American dream. *Critical Perspectives on Accounting, 12*(4), 501–525.

Miller, P. B. W., & Redding, R. (1986). *The FASB: The people, the process, and the politics.* Homewood, IL: Richard D. Irwin.

Mueller, G. G. (1967). *International accounting, part I.* New York: Macmillan.

Nair, R. D., & Frank, W. G. (1980). The impact of disclosure and measurement practices on international accounting classification. *The Accounting Review, 55*(3), 426–450.

Nederveen Pieterse, J. (2004). *Globalization or empire?* New York: Routledge.

Nobes, C. (1983). A judgmental international classification of financial reporting practices. *Journal of Business Finance and Accounting, 10*(1), 1–20.

Nobes, C. (2006). The survival of international differences under IFRS: Towards a research agenda. *Accounting and Business Research, 36*(3), 233–245

Nobes, C. (2008). Accounting classification in the IFRS era. *Australian Accounting Review, 18*(3), 191–198.

Nobes, C. (2011). IFRS practices and the persistence of accounting system classification. *Abacus, 47*(3), 267–283.

Nobes, C. (2015). IFRS ten years on: Has the IASB imposed extensive use of fair value? Has the EU learnt to love IFRs? And does the use of fair value make IFRS illegal in the EU? *Accounting in Europe, 12*(2), 153–170.

Nobes, C., & Parker, R. (2017). *Comparative international accounting.* 13th ed. Harlow, UK: Pearson.

Nobes, C., & Stadler, C. (2013). How arbitrary are international accounting classification? Lessons from centuries of classifying in many disciplines, and experiments with IFRS data. *Accounting, Organizations and Society, 38,* 573–595.

Noguchi, M., & Boyns, T. (2012). The development of budgets and their use for purpose of control in Japanese aviation, 1928–1945: The role of the state. *Accounting, Auditing & Accountability Journal, 25*(3), 416–451.

Noguchi, Y. (1998). The 1940 system: Japan under the wartime economy. *American Economic Review, 88*(2), 404–407.

Oe, K. (1995). *Japan, the ambiguous, and myself: The Nobel Prize speech and other lectures.* Tokyo: Kodansha International.

Oliver, C. (1991). Strategic responses to institutional processes. *Academy of Management Review, 16*(1), 145–179.

Peirce, C. S. (1955). *Philosophical writing of Peirce.* New York: Dover Publications.

Peltzman, S. (1976). Towards a more general theory of regulation. *Journal of Law and Economics* (August), 211–240.

Peng, S., & Bewley, K. (2010). Adaptability to fair value accounting in an emerging economy: A case study of China's IFRS convergence. *Accounting, Auditing & Accountability Journal, 23*(8), 982–1011.

Perry, J., & Nölke, A. (2005). International accounting standard setting: A network approach. *Business & Politics, 7*(3), Article 5.

Pigou, A. (1932). *The economics of welfare.* London: Macmillan.

Pope, P. F., & McLeay, S. J. (2011). The European IFRS experiment: Objectives, research challenges and some early evidence. *Accounting and Business Research*, *41*(3), 233–266.

Posner, R. (1974). Theories of economic regulation. *Bell Journal of Economic and Management Science*, *5*, 335–358.

Previts, G., & Merino, B. D. (1998). *A history of accountancy in the United States: The cultural significance of accounting*. Columbus, OH: Ohio State University Press.

Ramanna, K. (2013). The international politics of IFRS harmonization. *Accounting, Economics and Law*, *3*(2), 1–46.

Ramanna, K. (2015). *Political accounting: Corporate interest, ideology, and leadership in the shaping of accounting rules for the market economy*. Chicago, IL: Chicago University Press.

Reay, T., & Jones, C. (2016). Qualitatively capturing institutional logics. *Strategic Organization*, *14*(4), 441–454.

Richardson, A. J. (1989). Corporatism and intraprofessional hegemony: A study of regulation and internal social order. *Accounting, Organizations and Society*, *14*(5–6), 415–431.

Richardson, A. J., & Eberlein, B. (2011). Legitimating transnational standard-setting: The case of the International Accounting Standards Board. *Journal of Business Ethics*, *98*, 217–245.

Richardson, A. J., & Kilfoyle, E. (2009). Regulation. In J. R. Edwards & S. P. Walker (Eds.), *The Routledge companion to accounting history* (pp. 317–338). New York: Routledge.

Robson, K. (1991). On the arena of accounting change: The process of translation. *Accounting, Organizations and Society*, *16*(5–6), 547–570.

Sakagami, M., Yoshimi, H., & Okano, H. (1999). Japanese accounting profession in transition. *Accounting, Auditing & Accountability Journal*, *13*(3), 340–357.

Sanada, M. (2018). The legal backing for accounting standard-setting in Japan: A historical review. *Accounting History*, *23*(3), *Special Issue: Histories of Accounting Standard-Setting*, 338–359. https://doi.org/10.1177/1032373217743022

Scott, D. R. (1931). *The cultural significance of accounts*. Lawrence, KS: Scholars Book Co. (reprinted in 1973)

Scott, W. R. (2014). *Institutions and organizations: Ideas, interests, and identities*. 4th ed. Thousand Oaks, CA: SAGE.

Soderstrom, N. S., & Sun, K. J. (2007). IFRS adoption and accounting quality: A review. *European Accounting Review*, *16*(4), 675–702.

Stigler, G. (1971). The theory of economic regulation. *Bell Journal of Economic and Management Science* (Spring), 2–21.

Suchman, M. C. (1995). Managing legitimacy: Strategic and institutional approaches. *Academy of Management Review*, *20*(3), 571–610.

Sunder, S. (2002). Regulatory competition among accounting standards within and across international boundaries. *Journal of Accounting and Public Policy*, *21*, 219–234.

Sunder, S. (2011). IFRS monopoly: The pied piper of financial reporting. *Accounting and Business Research*, *41*(3), 291–306.

Suzuki, T. (2012). *Oxford report: The impact of IFRS on wider stakeholders of socio-economy in Japan.* Retrieved from www.fsa.go.jp/common/about/research/20120614.html

Tamm Hallström, K. (2004). *Organizing international standardization: ISO and the IASC in quest of authority.* Cheltenham, UK: Edward Elgar.

Thornton, P. H., Ocasio, W., & Lounsbury, M. (2012). *The institutional logics perspective: A new approach to culture, structure, and process.* Oxford, UK: Oxford University Press.

Tinker, T. (1984). Theories of the state and the state of accounting: Economic reductionism and political voluntarism in accounting regulation theory. *Journal of Accounting and Public Policy, 3,* 55–74.

Trevor, M. (2001). Is Japan changing? In A. Holzhausen (Ed.), *Can Japan globalize? Studies on Japan's changing political economy and the process of globalization in honor of Sung-Jo Park* (pp. 3–17). Berlin: Springer.

Tsumori, T. (1995). Development of a "philosophy of disclosure" in accounting institution in Japan. In A. Tsuji & P. Garner (Eds.), *Studies in accounting history: Tradition and innovation for the twenty-first century* (pp. 71–92). Westport, CT: Greenwood Press.

Tsunogaya, N. (2016). Issues affecting decisions on mandatory adoption of International Financial Reporting Standards (IFRS) in Japan. *Accounting, Auditing & Accountability Journal, 29*(5), 828–860.

Tsunogaya, N., & Tokuga, Y. (2015). Controversies over the development of Japanese Modified International Standards (JMIS). *Korean Accounting Review, 40*(2), 299–335.

Tudor, A. T. (2013). Balancing the public and the private interest: A dilemma of accounting profession. *Procedia – Social and Behavioral Sciences, 92,* 930–935.

United Nations Conference on Trade and Development (UNCTAD). (2008). *Practical implementation of International Financial Reporting Standards: Lessons learned.* New York and Geneva: United Nations.

Wallace, R., & Meek, G. (2002). Contributions we seek to publish. *Journal of International Accounting Research, 1,* 1–2.

Walton, P. (2015). IFRS in Europe: An observer's perspective of the next 10 years. *Accounting in Europe, 12*(2), 135–151.

Watts, R. L., & Zimmerman, J. L. (1978). Towards a positive theory of the determination of accounting standards. *The Accounting Review, 53*(1), 112–134.

Watts, R. L., & Zimmerman, J. L. (1986). *Positive accounting theory.* Englewood Cliffs: Prentice Hall.

Weber, M. (1946). Science as a vocation. In H. H. Gerth & C. W. Mills (trans. and Ed.), *From Max Weber: Essays in sociology.* New York: Oxford University Press.

Westney, D. E. (1987). *Imitation and innovation: The transfer of western organizational patterns to Meiji Japan.* Cambridge, MA: Harvard University Press.

Williamson, O. E. (1985). *The economic institutions of capitalism.* New York: The Free Press.

Yin, R. K. (2018). *Case study research and applications: Design and methods,* Sixth edition. London, UK: SAGE.

Yonekura, A., Gallhofer, S., & Haslam, J. (2012). Accounting disclosure, corporate governance and the battle for markets: The case of trade negotiations between Japan and U.S. *Critical Perspectives on Accounting, 23*, 312–331.

Zeff, S. A. (2003). How the U.S. accounting profession got where it is today: Part I. *Accounting Horizons, 17*(3), 189–205.

Zimmermann, J., Werner, J., & Volmer, P. B. (2008). *Global governance in accounting rebalancing public power and private commitment.* Basingstoke: Palgrave Macmillan.

In Japanese

Chiba, J. (2012). Accounting standards and business accounting system in Japan. In J. Chiba & T. Nakano (Eds.), *History of accounting and accounting study* (pp. 451–483). Tokyo: Chuokeizai-sha.

Endo, H., Komiyama, S., Sakase, S., Tagaya, M., & Hashimoto, T. (2015). *Japanese corporate accounting history after World War II.* Tokyo: Chuokeizai-sha.

Hiramatsu, K. (2015). International standardization and the future of accounting system/research. *Bulletin of Japanese Association for International Accounting Studies, 38*(2), 63–78.

Ishikawa, J. (2006). *Changes in society and accounting.* Tokyo: Nippon Hyoron-sha.

Ito, K. (2013). Current situation, issues, and future challenges of the IFRS implementation in Japan. *Reconstruction of Financial Accounting System* (special issue of *Accounting*, November 2013), 2–19.

Kyougoku, J. (1987). *Japanese-style versus western-style.* Tokyo: University of Tokyo Press.

Matsumoto, T. (2009). Internationalization of accounting standards and the status of Japan. *Doshisha University World Business Review, 10*, 183–186.

Mitsui, H. (2009). The application of International Financial Reporting Standards in Japanese companies. *Accounting, 61*(9),113–120.

Miyauchi, T., & Tokuga, Y. (2007). International accounting and the Japanese accounting big-bang. In R. Kabata & T. Yui (Eds.), *Modern Accounting and the Japanese Accounting Big Bang* (pp. 240–249). Tokyo: Moriyama-Shoten.

Mori, J. (2017). Politicization of the accounting for asset impairment in Japan. *Accounting, 69*(3), 61–65.

Nishikawa, I. (2007). The ASBJ's strategy toward the global convergence of accounting standards: Announcement of the Tokyo Agreement. *Accounting Standards & Disclosure Quarterly, 18*(September 2007), 12–15.

Nishikawa, I. (2014). Accounting standards and laws. *Aoyama Accounting Review, 4*, 69–73.

Noguchi, Y. (2010). *The 1940 system: Japan under the wartime economy.* Extended ed. Tokyo: Toyo Keizai. (originally published in 1995)

Oishi, K. (2007). Accounting regulation and accounting big bang in Japan. In R. Kabata & T. Yui (Eds.), *Modern accounting and the Japanese accounting Big Ban* (pp. 240–249). Tokyo: Moriyama-Shoten.

Saito, S. (Ed.). (2004). *Kommentar: Accounting standards for business combination.* Tokyo: Chuokeizai-sha.

Saito, S. (2009). *Research in accounting standards.* Tokyo: Chuokeizai-sha.

Saito, S. (2014). *Introduction to corporate accounting.* Tokyo: Yuhikaku Publishing.

Sawabe, N. (2005). *Accounting reformation and risk society.* Tokyo: Iwanami Shoten.

Special Committee of Japan Accounting Association (JAA Special Committee). (2008). *Changes in financial reporting: Interim report.* Tokyo: JAA.

Sugimoto, T. (2009). Accounting standard setting and IFRS. *Issues in the Implementation of IFRS* (special issue of *Accounting,* 2009), 80–96.

Tokuga, Y. (2000). *International accounting: Difference and harmony.* Tokyo: Chuokeizai-sha.

Tokuga, Y. (2012a). *The impact of IFRS on the Japanese business.* Seminar Report 2011 of Kansai University Institute of Economics and Political Studies, 117–128.

Tokuga, Y. (2012b). A study on the mixed accounting models: Income model or net assets model. *Financial Research, 2012/7,* 141–203.

Tokuga, Y. (2015). Problems with mandatory adoption of IFRS in Japan: "What" and "why"? *Aoyama Accounting Review, 5,* 72–79.

Tsujiyama, E. (2014). Issues in Japan's Modified International Standards. *Accounting (Kigyo-Kaikei), 66*(11), 35–44.

Tsujiyama, E. (2015). Theoretical challenges of International Financial Reporting Standards (IFRS) and future prospects. In E. Tsujiyama (Ed.), *Accounting thought in IFRS: Past, present and future prospects* (pp. 1–34). Tokyo: Chuokeizai-sha.

Tsumori, T. (2002). *Logic of accounting standard-setting.* Tokyo: Chuokeizai-sha.

Usui, A. (2015). *Economic analysis of accounting institutions.* Tokyo: Chuokeizai-sha.

Watabe, R. (2015). The activities of the Standards Advisory Council. *Accounting Standards & Disclosure Quarterly, 49*(June 2015), 13–34.

Yamaji, H., Suzuki, K., Kajiwara, A., & Matsumoto, Y. (1994) *The Formation of Business Accounting System in Japan.* Tokyo: Chuokeizai-sha.

Primary sources

Accounting Standards Board of Japan (ASBJ). (2005). *Comments on draft memorandum of understanding on the role of accounting standard-setters and their relationships with the International Accounting Standards Board (IASB).* Tokyo: ASBJ.

Accounting Standards Board of Japan (ASBJ). (2006a). *Statement on Japan's progress toward convergence between Japanese GAAP and IFRSs–In reference to technical advice on equivalence by CESR.* Tokyo: ASBJ.

Accounting Standards Board of Japan (ASBJ). (2006b). *Press release: The ASBJ and the IASB hold third meeting on joint project towards convergence.* March 2, 2006. Tokyo: ASBJ.

Accounting Standards Board of Japan (ASBJ). (2006c). *Project plan concerning the development of Japanese accounting standards: Initiatives towards the international convergence of accounting standards in light of the equivalence assessment by the EU.* October 12, 2006. Tokyo: ASBJ.

Accounting Standards Board of Japan (ASBJ). (2007a). *Press release: The ASBJ and the IASB announce Tokyo Agreement on achieving convergence of accounting standards by 2011.* August 8, 2007. Tokyo: ASBJ.

Accounting Standards Board of Japan (ASBJ). (2007b). *Press release: Release of project plan: Initiatives toward international convergence of accounting standards based on the Tokyo Agreement.* December 6, 2007. Tokyo: ASBJ.

Accounting Standards Board of Japan (ASBJ). (2011). *Comments on request for views, agenda consultation 2011.* November 30, 2011. Tokyo: ASBJ.

Accounting Standards Board of Japan (ASBJ). (2012). *Re: Invitation to comment "proposal to establish an Accounting Standards Advisory Forum".* December 17, 2012. Tokyo: ASBJ.

Accounting Standards Board of Japan (ASBJ). (2013). *Due Process for the development of Japanese GAAP and Japan's Modified International Standards (Due Process Rules).* June 14, 2013. Tokyo: ASBJ.

Accounting Standards Board of Japan (ASBJ). (2014). *Exposure draft on "Japan's Modified International Standards (JMIS): Accounting standards comprising IFRSs and the ASBJ modifications".* July 31, 2014. Tokyo: ASBJ.

Accounting Standards Board of Japan (ASBJ). (2015a). *Japan's Modified International Standards (JMIS): Accounting standards comprising IFRSs and the ASBJ modifications.* June 30, 2015. Tokyo: ASBJ.

Accounting Standards Board of Japan (ASBJ). (2015b). Recognition criteria in the conceptual framework. *ASBJ short paper series no. 2: Conceptual framework.* November 2015. Tokyo: ASBJ.

Accounting Standards Board of Japan (ASBJ). (2015c). *Re: Comments on request for views: Trustees' review of structure and effectiveness: Issues for the review.* November 30, 2015. Tokyo: ASBJ.

Accounting Standards Board of Japan (ASBJ). (2015d). *Comments on request for views: 2015 agenda consultation.* December 25, 2015. Tokyo: ASBJ.

Accounting Standards Board of Japan (ASBJ). (2015e). *Re: Comments on request for views: 2015 agenda consultation.* December 25, 2015. Tokyo: ASBJ.

Accounting Standards Board of Japan (ASBJ). (2016). *Comments on exposure draft – Trustees' review of structure and effectiveness: Proposed amendments to the IFRS Foundation Constitution.* September 15, 2016. Tokyo: ASBJ.

Accounting Standards Board of Japan/Financial Accounting Standards Foundation (ASBJ/FASF). (2012). *ASBJ/FASF 10 years history.* Tokyo: ASBJ.

Business Accounting Council of Japan (BAC). (2009). *Opinion on the application of International Financial Reporting Standards (IFRS) in Japan (Interim Report).* June 30, 2009. Tokyo: Japan.

Business Accounting Council of Japan (BAC). (2012). *Discussion summary for the consideration on the application of IFRS in Japan (Discussion Summary).* July 2, 2012. Tokyo: Japan.

Business Accounting Council of Japan (BAC). (2013). *The present policy of the application of International Financial Reporting Standards (IFRS).* June 20, 2013. Tokyo: Japan.

Cabinet Office of Japan (COJ). (2013). *Japan revitalization strategy: Japan is back.* June 14, 2013. Tokyo: Cabinet Office.

Cabinet Office of Japan (COJ). (2014). *Japan revitalization strategy – Revised in 2014: Japan's challenge for the future.* June 24, 2014. Tokyo: Cabinet Office.

Committee of European Securities Regulators (CESR). (2004). *Final concept paper on equivalence of certain third country GAAP and on description of certain third countries mechanisms of enforcement of financial information.* December 2004. Paris: CESR.

Committee of European Securities Regulators (CESR). (2005). *Technical advice on equivalence of certain third country GAAP and on description of certain third countries mechanisms of enforcement of financial information.* June 2005. Paris: CESR.

Committee of European Securities Regulators (CESR). (2007). *Consultation paper: CESR's advice on the equivalence of Chinese, Japanese and US GAAPs.* December 2007. Paris: CESR.

European Commission (EC). (2002). *Regulation (EC) No. 1606/2002 of the European Parliament and of the Council of 19 July 2002 on the application of international accounting standards.* Brussel: EC.

European Commission (EC). (2007). *First report to the European Securities Committee and to the European Parliament on convergence between International Financial Reporting Standards (IFRS) and third country national Generally Accepted Accounting Principles (GAAPs).* July 2007. Brussel: EC.

Financial Service Agency of Japan (FSA). (2015). *IFRS adoption report.* April 15, 2015. Tokyo: FSA.

G20. (2008). *Declaration summit on financial markets and the world economy.* November 15, 2008, Washington, DC.

Japan Leasing Association (JLA). (2003). *Disclosure of lease information and impacts of abolishment of "off-balance sheet treatment".* Special study on revision of lease accounting standards.

Jimi, S. (2011). *Considerations on the application of IFRS.* June 21, 2011. Tokyo: FSA.

Keidanren (Japan Federation of Economic Organizations). (2003). *Seeking international collaboration on accounting standards.* October 21, 2003. Tokyo: Nippon Keidanren. Retrieved from www.keidanren.or.jp/english/policy/2003/096/proposal.html

Keidanren (Japan Federation of Economic Organizations). (2006). *Nippon Keidanren supports to accelerate the convergence of accounting standards and to seek mutual recognition of standards in Japan, the United States, and Europe.* June 20, 2006. Tokyo: Nippon Keidanren. Retrieved from www.keidanren.or.jp/english/policy/2006/043.html

Keidanren (Japan Federation of Economic Organizations). (2008a). *Summary of results of questionnaire survey of Japan's future corporate accounting system.* August 8, 2008. Tokyo: Nippon Keidanren. Retrieved from www.keidanren.or.jp/english/policy/2007/064.html

Keidanren (Japan Federation of Economic Organizations). (2008b). *Advancing the convergence of accounting standards.* August 8, 2008. Tokyo: Nippon Keidanren. Retrieved from www.keidanren.or.jp/english/policy/2007/064.html

Keidanren (Japan Federation of Economic Organizations). (2008c). *Future directions of accounting standards in Japan: The next step towards a single set of accounting standards.* October 14, 2008. Tokyo: Nippon Keidanren.

Keidanren (Japan Federation of Economic Organizations). (2013). *Basic stance on Japan's future corporate accounting system.* June 10, 2013. Tokyo: Nippon Keidanren. Keidanren (Japan Federation of Economic Organizations). (2017). *Charter of corporate behavior (provisional translation).* November 8, 2017. Tokyo: Nippon Keidanren.

Keidanren (Japan Federation of Economic Organizations), the Japanese Institute of Certified Public Accountants, Tokyo Stock Exchanges, Japan Securities Dealers Association, Japanese Bankers Association, the Life Insurance Association of Japan, the Marine & Fire Insurance Association of Japan, Inc., the Japan Chamber of Commerce & Industry, the Security Analysts Association of Japan, & Corporation Finance Research Institute, Japan. (2001). *Establishment of the Financial Accounting Standards Foundation.* July 27, 2001. Retrieved from www.asb.or.jp/en/fasf-asbj/overview.html

Keidanren (Japan Federation of Economic Organizations), the Japanese Institute of Certified Public Accountants, Tokyo Stock Exchanges, Japan Securities Dealers Association, Japanese Bankers Association, the Life Insurance Association of Japan, the Marine & Fire Insurance Association of Japan, Inc., the Japan Chamber of Commerce & Industry, & the Security Analysts Association of Japan. (2002). *About the status (applicability) of accounting standards and other guidance issued by the Accounting Standards Board of Japan/Financial Accounting Standards Foundation.* May 17, 2002.

Keidanren, & Union des Industries de la Communauté Européenne (UNICE). (2004). *Joint statement on international accounting standards.* April 19, 2004. Tokyo: Nippon Keidanren. Retrieved from www.keidanren.or.jp/english/policy/2004/032.html

Liberal Democratic Party of Japan (LDP). (2013). *Statement on approach to IFRS.* June 13, 2013. Tokyo: LDP.

Liberal Democratic Party of Japan (LDP). (2014). *Japan revival vision.* May 23, 2014. Tokyo: LDP.

Ministry of Foreign Affairs of Japan (MOFA). (1997). *Joint statement on the U.S.-Japan enhanced initiative on deregulation and competition policy.* June 19, 1997. Tokyo: MOFA.

Ministry of Foreign Affairs of Japan (MOFA). (1999). *Second joint status report on the U.S.-Japan enhanced initiative on deregulation and competition policy.* May 3, 1999. Tokyo: MOFA.

Mitsui, H. (2009). The application of IFRS by Japanese companies. *Accounting (Special Issue 'Issues concerning the application of IFRS'),* 2–11.

Nihon Keizai Shimbun (Nikkei). (2017). *A rush of delisting from NYSE.* March 9, 2017. Retrieved from www.nikkei.com/article/DGXLASDZ09HRM_Z00C17A3000000/

Retrieved from www.keidanren.or.jp/en/policy/2013/056.html

Retrieved from www.keidanren.or.jp/en/policy/csr/charter.html

Retrieved from www.keidanren.or.jp/english/policy/2008/071.html

SEC. (2007). *Acceptance from foreign private issuers of financial statements prepared in accordance with International Financial Reporting Standards without reconciliation to U.S. GAAP.* Washington, DC: SEC.

SEC. (2008). *Concept release on allowing U.S. issuers to prepare financial statements prepared in accordance with International Financial Reporting Standards.* Washington, DC: SEC.

SEC. (2010). *Commission statement in support of convergence and global accounting standards.* [Release Nos. 33-9109; 34-61578]. Washington, DC: SEC.

ASBJ statement

ASBJ Guidance No. 16 *Guidance on accounting standards for lease transactions*, March 30, 2007.

ASBJ Statement No. 13 *Accounting standards for lease transactions*, March 30, 2007.

Websites

Accounting Standards Board of Japan/Financial Accounting Standards Foundation (ASBJ/FASF). Retrieved September 30, 2017 from www.asb.or.jp

Financial Services Agency of Japan (FSA). Retrieved September 30, 2017 from www.fsa.go.jp

IAS Plus. Retrieved September 30, 2017 from www.iasplus.com

IFRS Foundation. Retrieved September 30, 2017 from www.ifrs.org

Japan Business Federation (Keidanren). Retrieved April 30, 2019 from www.keidanren.or.jp

Japan Business Federation (Keidanren). Retrieved September 30, 2017 from www.keidanren.or.jp

Japanese Institute of Certified Public Accountants (JICPA). Retrieved September 30, 2017 from www.hp.jicpa.or.jp

Japan Exchange Group (JEG). Retrieved September 30, 2017 from www.jpx.co.jp

Ministry of Foreign Affairs of Japan (MOFA). Retrieved April 30, 2019 from www.mofa.go.jp

Securities Analysts Association of Japan (SAAJ). Retrieved September 30, 2017 from www.saa.or.jp

Appendices

Appendix A

The sequence of events surrounding the ASBJ, the convergence between IFRS and Japanese GAAP, and related documents

Year/Month	Events/documents	Issuer(s) or relating organization(s)
March 2001	*A Proposal for Better Corporate Accounting*	Nippon Keidanren
April 2001	Establishment of the International Accounting Standards Board (IASB)	Keidanren, JICPA, Tokyo Stock Exchanges, Japan Securities Dealers Association, Japanese Bankers Association, The Life Insurance Association of Japan, The Marine & Fire Insurance Association of Japan, Inc., The Japan Chamber of Commerce & Industry, The Security Analysts Association of Japan, and CFRI
July 2001	Establishment of the Financial Accounting Standards Foundation (FASF)	
August 2001	The first board meeting of the Accounting Standards Board of Japan (ASBJ)	

(*Continued*)

(Continued)

Year/Month	Events/documents	Issuer(s) or relating organization(s)
May 2002	*About the Status (Applicability) of Accounting Standards and Other Guidance Issued by the Accounting Standards Board of Japan / Financial Accounting Standards Foundation*	Keidanren, JICPA, Tokyo Stock Exchanges, Japan Securities Dealers Association, Japanese Bankers Association, The Life Insurance Association of Japan, The Marine & Fire Insurance Association of Japan, Inc., The Japan Chamber of Commerce & Industry, and The Security Analysts Association of Japan
October 2002	*Memorandum of Understanding "The Norwalk Agreement"*	IASB/FASB
April 2003	The Liberal Democratic Party (LDP) announced its intention to submit a private member's bill that required to suspend the implementation of the mark-to-market accounting for five years and accounting for impairment of fixed assets for two years.	
June 2003	*About the Outcome of the Emergency Deliberations Regarding the Application of the Mark-to-Marketing of / Mandatorily Writing-Down Securities and the Effective Date for the Impairment Accounting for Fixed Assets*	ASBJ
October 200	*Seeking International Collaboration on Accounting Standards*	Nippon Keidanren
April 2004	*Joint Statement on International Accounting Standards*	UNICE/Nippon Keidanren
June 2004	*Report on the Internationalization of Business Accounting in Japan*	Ministry of Economy, Trade and Industry of Japan (METI)
July 2004	*Medium-Term Operation Policy* (July 2004)	ASBJ
March 2005	The ASBJ and the IASB held the initial meeting on joint project for convergence (**Convergence Project with the IASB**). – Since then, they shall have biannual meetings in Tokyo and London alternatively.	IASB/ASBJ

Year/Month	Events/documents	Issuer(s) or relating organization(s)
July 2005	*Technical Advice on Equivalence of Certain Third Country GAAP and on Description of Certain Third Countries Mechanisms of Enforcement of Financial Information* – Identified 26 major technical differences between Japanese GAAP and IFRS.	CESR
January 2006	*Statement on Japan's Progress toward Convergence between Japanese GAAP and IFRSs – In Reference to Technical Advice on Equivalence by CESR*	ASBJ
February 2006	*A Roadmap for Convergence between IFRSs and US GAAP – 2006–2008 Memorandum of Understanding between the FASB and the IASB*	IASB/FASB
May 2006	The ASBJ and the FASB held the first regular meeting in pursuit of global convergence between. – Since then, they shall have biannual meetings in Tokyo and Norwalk alternatively.	ASBJ/FASB
June 2006	*Nippon Keidanren Supports to Accelerate the Convergence of Accounting Standards and to Seek Mutual Recognition of Standards in Japan, the United States, and Europe*	Nippon Keidanren
July 200	*Basic Policies for Economic and Fiscal Management and Structural Reform 2006*	Japanese Government
July 2006	*Towards the International Convergence of Accounting Standards*	BAC (BADC)
October 2006	*Project Plan Concerning the Development of Japanese Accounting Standards – Initiatives towards the international convergence of accounting standards in light of the equivalence assessment by the EU*	ASBJ
April 2007	Chairman of the ASBJ was changed from Shizuki Saito to Ikuo Nishikawa.	

(*Continued*)

(Continued)

Year/Month	Events/documents	Issuer(s) or relating organization(s)
June 2007	*Medium-Term Operation Policy (June 2007)*	ASBJ
July 2007	The EC published a report on the work underway in Canada, Japan, and the United States on convergence between their national GAAP and IFRS used in the EU.	EC
August 2007	*Agreement on initiative to accelerate the convergence of accounting standards* – The ASBJ and the IASB announced Tokyo Agreement on achieving convergence of accounting standards by 2011.	IASB/ASBJ
August 2007	*Advancing the Convergence of Accounting Standards*	Nippon Keidanren
August 2007	*Concept Release on Allowing U.S. Issuers to Prepare Financial Statements in Accordance with International Financial Reporting Standards*	SEC
December 2007	*Acceptance from Foreign Private Issuers of Financial Statements Prepared in Accordance with International Financial Reporting Standards without Reconciliation to U.S. GAAP*	SEC
December 2007	*Release of Project Plan – Initiatives toward international convergence of accounting standards based on the Tokyo Agreement* – Since then, the project plan was modified accordingly.	ASBJ
March 2008	*Consultation Paper: CESR's advice on the equivalence of Chinese, Japanese and US GAAPs* – CESR issued the advice to the EC that Japanese GAAP were equivalent with IFRS on the condition that the ASBJ would assemble relevant accounting standards as planned in its project plan.	CESR

Year/Month	Events/documents	Issuer(s) or relating organization(s)
October 2008	The IASB issued *Reclassification of Financial Assets*, amendments of IAS 39 and IFRS 7, without normal due process.	IASB
October 2008	*Future Directions of Accounting Standards in Japan: The Next Step Towards a Single Set of Accounting Standards*	Nippon Keidanren
November 2008	The US SEC released "roadmap" to adopting IFRS for US firms.	SEC
December 2008	*Press Release: ASBJ completes the short-term projects in the Tokyo Agreement*	ASBJ
December 2008	The EC declared that Japanese GAAP were equivalent with IFRS similar to US GAAP.	EC
June 2009	*Opinion on the Application of International Financial Reporting Standards (IFRS) in Japan* (**Interim Report**)	BAC (BADC)
June 2009	The FSA proposed the revision of relevant Ordinance, Guidelines, and Public Notice. – The FSA approved these proposals in December.	FSA
July 2009	IFRS Council, a private sector committee to deliberate the IFRS application in Japan, was established under initiative of the FSA and ASBJ/FASF	
November 2009	The first meeting of the Asian-Oceanian Standard-Setters Group (AOSSG), a group of accounting standard-setters in Asian-Oceanian region, was held in Kuala Lumpur.	
February 2010	The SEC announced a partial suspension of IFRS roadmap.	SEC
June 2010	*Medium-Term Operation Policy* (June 2010)	ASBJ
May 2011	*Request for the application of IFRS in Japan*	Representatives of major Japanese companies
June 2011	Action Policies 2012–2013	Japanese Trade Union Confederation (*Rengo*)

(Continued)

Year/Month	Events/documents	Issuer(s) or relating organization(s)
June 2011	*Considerations on the Application of IFRS*	Shozaburo Jimi, Minister for Financial Services
November 2011	*Comments on Request for Views, Agenda Consultation 2011*	ASBJ (Council for Agenda Consultation of the IASB)
July 2012	*Discussion Summary for the Consideration on the Application of IFRS in Japan (**Discussion Summary**)*	BAC (BADC)
July 2012	The SEC issued the final staff report.	SEC
April 2013	The first meeting of the ASAF	IASB
June 2013	*Basic Stance on Japan's Future Corporate Accounting System*	Nippon Keidanren
June 2013	*Statement on Approach to IFRS*	LDP's Policy Research Council and the Business Accounting Sub-Committee
June 2013	*The Present Policy on the Application of International Financial Reporting Standards (IFRS) (**Present Policy**)*	BAC (BADC)
October 2013	Revision of Ordinance on terminology, forms, and preparation methods of consolidated financial statements.	FSA
March 2014	Revision of Ordinance on terminology, forms, and preparation methods of financial statements.	FSA
April 2014	ASBJ chairman changed to Yukio Ono	ASBJ
May 2014	*Japan Revival Vision*	LDP
June 2014	*Japan Revitalization Strategy (Revised in 2014) – Japan's challenge for the future*	Prime Minister of Japan and his Cabinet
July 2014	*Exposure Draft on Japan's Modified International Standards (JMIS): Accounting Standards Comprising IFRSs and the ASBJ Modification.*	ASBJ
April 2015	*IFRS Adoption Report*	FSA

Year/Month	Events/documents	Issuer(s) or relating organization(s)
June 2015	*Japan's Modified International Standards (JMIS): Accounting Standards Comprising IFRSs and the ASBJ Modifications* (including *Application of 'Japan's Modified International Standards; ASBJ Modification Accounting Standard No.1 Accounting for Goodwill*; and *ASBJ Modification Accounting Standard No. 2 Accounting for Other Comprehensive Income*)	ASBJ

Appendix B

List of ASBJ Statements/Accounting Standards (as of December 2015)

Number	ASBJ Statement/Accounting Standards	Date of issue*
1	Accounting Standard for Treasury Shares and Appropriation of Legal Reserve	2/21/2002 (3/26/2015)
2	Accounting Standard for Earnings Per Share	9/25/2002 (9/13/2013)
3	Partial Amendments to Accounting Standard for Retirement Benefits** – Replaced by ASBJ Statement No. 26 issued on May 17, 2017	3/16/2005
4	Accounting Standard for Directors' Bonus	11/29/2005
5	Accounting Standard for Presentation of Net Assets in the Balance Sheet	12/9/2005 (9/13/2013)
6	Accounting Standard for Statement of Changes in Net Assets	12/27/2005 (9/13/2013)
7	Accounting Standard for Business Divestitures	12/27/2005 (9/13/2013)
8	Accounting Standard for Share-based Payment	12/27/2005 (9/13/2013)
9	Accounting Standard for Measurement of Inventories	7/5/2006 (9/26/2008)
10	Accounting Standard for Financial Instruments**	8/11/2006 (3/10/2008)
11	Accounting Standard for Related Party Disclosures	10/17/2006 (12/26/2008)
12	Accounting Standard for Quarterly Financial Reporting	3/14/2007 (5/16/2014)
13	Accounting Standard for Lease Transactions	3/30/2007
14	Partial Amendments to Accounting Standard for Retirement Benefit (Part 2) – Replaced by ASBJ Statement No. 26 issued on May 17, 2017	5/15/2007

Number	ASBJ Statement/Accounting Standards	Date of issue*
15	Accounting Standard for Construction Contracts	12/27/2007
16	Accounting Standard for Equity Method of Accounting for Investments	3/10/2008 (3/26/2015)
17	Accounting Standard for Disclosure about Segments of Enterprise	3/21/2008 (9/13/2013)
18	Accounting Standard for Asset Retirement Obligations	3/31/2008 (5/17/2012)
19	Partial Amendments to Accounting Standard for Retirement Benefit (Part 3) – Replaced by ASBJ Statement No. 26 issued on May 17, 2017	7/31/2008
20	Accounting Standard for Disclosure about Fair Value of Investment and Rental Property	11/28/2008 (3/25/2011)
21	Accounting Standard for Business Combinations**	12/26/2008 (9/13/2013)
22	Accounting Standard for Consolidated Financial Statements	12/26/2008 (9/13/2013)
23	Partial Amendments to Accounting Standard for Research and Development Costs**	12/26/2008
24	Accounting Standard for Accounting Changes and Error Corrections	12/4/2009
25	Accounting Standard for Presentation of Comprehensive Income	6/30/2010 (9/13/2013)
26	Accounting Standard for Retirement Benefits	5/17/2012

* Figures between brackets indicate the last revision date.
** Original standards were issued by the BADC.

Source: ASBJ/FASF website.

Appendix C

Japanese Prime Minister (1996–2015)

Name	Term	Ruling Party
Ryutaro Hashimoto	January 1996–July 1998	LDP
Keizo Obuchi	July 1998–April 2000	LDP
Yoshiro Mori	April 2000–April 2001	LDP
Junichiro Koizumi	April 2001–September 2006	LDP
Shinzo Abe	September 2006–September 2007	LDP
Yasuo Fukuda	September 2007–September 2008	LDP
Taro Aso	September 2008–September 2009	LDP
Yukio Hatoyama	September 2009–June 2010	Democratic Party
Naoto Kan	June 2010–September 2011	Democratic Party
Yoshihiko Noda	September 2011–December 2012	Democratic Party
Shinzo Abe (2nd term)	December 2012–	LDP

Source: Authors.

Index

Printed in the United States
by Baker & Taylor Publisher Services